Table of Contents

This book is dedicated to the People, for they have yearned for freedom and equality for too long.

" Those who have to obtain power through corruption will use that power corruptly."
-Noah Plumb

Preface

In the month of November, 2016 in the year of our Lord, an event would take place that would remove all sense and sanity from mankind. The United States of America elected a Republican President, and Republicans maintained control of the House of Representatives, and the Senate. Those were the governing bodies that ran our old country, the United States of America. It is my prayer, that these words that I am writing, attached with this dictionary and Holy Bible, would find value in the context of what feels more like a last will than an accounting of the circumstances that led to the destruction of planet Earth. My wishes that any surviving human beings that possibly survived, will finally learn from the lessons of history, and not progress again to the times that are our current living conditions.

I

My story will begin here.
Having devoted my life to studying the history of mankind, one thing has remained constant, those who do not know their history are damned to repeat it. This has been my mantra from the beginning of my education, from student to teacher. I have taught this philosophy and given parallels from civilization to civilization on how those that do not apply this mindset have always fallen victim to their destruction by refusing to learn from the mistakes of others. Well, the United States was no different.

My last job was at Duke University, located in Durham, North Carolina, where I was a tenured professor teaching history, this would not be my last time. I never believed in the traditional methods of teaching, having students memorize dates, names and places as if that knowledge was supposed to carry them to a fulfilling and successful life. The old form of passing on lessons of life we need to know fell on deaf ears mostly because it was boring and very little of the intended message got through to students. I always felt that the best and most efficient method of conveying the true meaning of any period covered, was to try and make the student walk in the shoes of that person or culture to truly understand the nature of what happened and why. This may be the last lesson I ever convey, and to whomever reads this, I hope it will give some insight on what not to do ever again. If you're a survivor please take heed to these lessons that led to the total destruction of mankind as we knew it.

Little did I know, the curriculum I decided to cover during my last teaching semester at Duke, would create such an uprising in my life and in this country.

As I strolled into my lecture hall, I had the thought process of a man determined to penetrate the veil that had been casted over our educational system; and inspire my classes to be empowered with the truth. Also, with a Presidential election rapidly approaching, and with the political polarization climate that exists, it was important to me to arm the next generation of voters, just how, to vote in their own best interest. As soon as I walked through the doors into my beautiful coliseum shaped classroom. Aw, how I miss that classroom, it wasn't traditional by any means. The bottom had a wooden oval for a teacher to stand on with an old 1950's chalkboard that I salvaged from the history department's storage unit. I wasn't going to let this relic sit idle for no reason, I was going to use it. All of the bleachers, yes bleachers, were of old mahogany wood, every week when my room was cleaned the janitor would use lemon pine sol to clean them and the smell permeated throughout the room. The room remained silent as the chatter began to subside, leaving only a few whispers. I paused as all of my students looked at me before I took a deep breath and walked down the stairs to the center of the coliseum. I walked down, amidst whispers and creaks from the old wood before I reached my standing place amongst the oval stage. I threw my leather Indiana Jones replica bag on the floor and walked up and swung the blackboard around to face me. I grabbed the chalk and walked up to the board and wrote one word in all caps "PILGRIMS". I turned and faced the class, let us begin.

II

...before the United States of America became a country of its own, it was discovered by what we used to call "The Pilgrims". The Pilgrims sailed to this land across a vast body of water called the Atlantic Ocean. They came in 1620, and they named the place they landed, Plymouth Rock. The entire reason they left their own country, England, was to escape religious persecution. The King of England, Henry VIII, at that time did not agree with the teachings of the Catholic Church, the predominant religion there, because he felt as king he should be able to divorce his wife because she bore him no son to pass the throne to. He felt, as men have since the beginning of time, that the male species was the dominant species and the heir to the throne should be a male. Since she did not give him a son to pass the throne to, he felt he was within his rights to divorce her and find a wife that would give him a son. The king formed his own church, the Anglican Church, and of course, ended up having multiple wives, ironically, none of them giving birth to a boy.

...now you were free to worship in any church you wanted, but your tax dollars went to support the king's church. This made many of the subjects in the kingdom upset, and the king punished those that voiced opposition to this rule and forced them to support his views, not taking into account any feelings the people had, as they were his to do with as he pleased. Basically, the rights of the people were ignored and this led to much discord in the kingdom.

Those that chose to search for a better life and not live under tyranny left on those initial boats that headed across the water not having any idea where they were going , or if, they would ultimately find land and a place to live free and peacefully. This must have been terrifying, crossing a body of water having no certainty that another hemisphere lay on the other side. I know I would have been terrified to be getting on a boat and heading to the unknown, not knowing what was on the other side. Also, consider what can happen in the middle of the ocean with no land in sight for weeks on end. I can only imagine it compares to the first space flight of John Glenn being the first man to orbit the earth. These Pilgrims were the cornerstone for the foundation of "separation of church and state". In other words, keep religion out of government.

This topic led to conversations about the idea of "less government", and why there should be no arms of government like the IRS, and the EPA, Department of Commerce, or whatever level of government you feel did not need to have authority over its citizens. This led to a great impromptu assignment. Pick a government agency, and research its origin, what services it provides and justify why you think this agency should go.
Our next session in class was a totally different one. The cries for the closure of government agencies was not the topic of discussion, but why those agencies exist and what the missions of those agencies are.

In the previous class, the biggest discussion on which agency to close was predominantly the IRS. The majority thought that any money earned was all theirs, and government was using its power in the most intrusive way, taking part of your paycheck. Shoot, they did no work for it, why should they get my money?

Those that actually did their research found why the IRS is probably one of the most important arms of government. Without the IRS, the government would have zero dollars in resources to:

1. Provide for the National Defense
2. Build hospitals
3. Build roads, bridges, dams, schools
4. Build airports and maintain airspace security
5. Provide for the general Health, Safety and Welfare of the Citizens of the United States of America.

I used the projector in my lecture hall, and placed that portion of the Constitution, on the wall behind me, depicting the responsibility Congress has to the people of the United States. I asked, "how is government supposed to keep its responsibilities to the people, if the people do not provide collectively to their government?"

One by one, each arm of government that students felt we could do without was substantiated to be justified. From the standpoint of having someone ensuring the water we drink, the food we eat, the air we breathe, there is a need for a watchdog making sure the interest of the people are a priority and not that of big money.

We talked about this theory of 'less government". Based on what the pilgrims came here for, less government meant not having to pay to support someone else's religion, while no one was mandated to financially support yours.

In our current political climate, there are those that claim to stand on the idea that less government means eliminating those arms of government put in place to perform their duties as prescribed by the aforementioned Constitution. They claim to stand on religious beliefs that those who do not believe as they do are the reason our country, my country, has turned to the "Dark Side". Those people are our elected Legislators in Washington D.C.

...they represent big money, and not the citizens that are negatively affected by the the laws they enact on behalf of big money. These laws have hugely had a negative impact the citizens of this country. To be fair, there are Democrats that are beholden to big money as well, Hillary Clinton being the prime example. It is well documented the money she receives from big money, and the laws that keep their best interest in mind. At least she is not hypocritical enough to stand on the Religious Platform.

...the foundation of the concept of Freedom of Religion, was that all people were free to worship without fear of retribution for their beliefs. Republicans on the far right side of normality today want to ban the religious beliefs of Islam in this country. Islam means "peace" in Arabic, and Muslim believers of the faith of Islam practice this peaceful religion daily, while being contributing members to our society. They serve in our Armed Forces, they are doctors that treat us, they are Public Safety personnel that serve in our communities. But those on the far right do not believe the First Amendment to our Constitution should apply to Muslims. Who was next, basically anyone that did not support White Republicans in charge of government.

Fast forward to present day, and I am on an island in the middle of that same Atlantic Ocean, trying to make sense of everything that happened while simultaneously coming to grips with my reality in the midst of this nuclear holocaust. How I got here is the real story because so many had no contingent plan for safety in case such an event as this happened, and most importantly, no one paid attention to history or heeded the advice and knowledge I tried to arm them with.

III

...have you ever heard the children's story called "Chicken Little"? (sometimes the easiest lessons are from children's books) Chicken Little was a fictional character that had an acorn fall from a tree and hit her on the head. She was so terrified because she was ignorant and thought the sky was falling, thus the reason for her paranoia. She ran frantically about screaming "the sky is falling" getting all her friends, neighbors and anyone that would listen to her story. Everyone believed her but a clever fox. The fox used this hysteria to capitalize on this, because Chicken Little and her group were his prey. The fox told all of them to listen to him, and rounded them all up in a place he told them they were safe. In reality, the fox herded the other dumb animals to a place where he could pick them off one by one and ate to his content. This is one of the many tactics used by the radical lawmakers on the right, fear. Fear can be a great motivator, and the right knew this. They played on the weak and stupid of this country to gain control of government. To fully understand how they used fear we have to address what laws were in place and why Republican lawmakers wanted them to change.

I know my plan over the course of the semester was to cover the political history of this country to current date, but I loved keeping things fresh. Nothing taught me better than keeping students guessing as to the lessons in the timeline we would cover. Since Americans had a general negativity toward the people of Iran, I decided to fast forward to 1979.

...the United States had an embassy in the country of Iran. This is not noteworthy in and of itself, because every country in the world had embassies in every country as well, as long as good relations were established between those countries. So, in 1979, the American Embassy was invaded, overthrown and occupied by the citizens of that country. America has not had an embassy there since. But the "Chicken Little" method was applied here. The media portrayed this event as a blatant and unprovoked attack on the United States. In reality, the United States Government, via the Central Intelligence Agency (CIA) wrongly imprisoned the elected leader of Iran, the Ayatollah Khomeini. This left sole power and authority of the Iranian government to the Shah, who was for the most part a puppet put in place to oversee that country for the purpose of having access to the rich oil fields that Iran possessed. When the Ayatollah was released after over twenty years of imprisonment, he led the overthrow of the United States embassy in that country. So, from the perspective of the Iranian people, they were only responding to the actions of the American government. Ever since, the American media portray Iran as the enemy. And the majority of Republican elected officials, and some Democrats, have beaten the drums of war against that country.

...from 2008, Senator John McCain(R) of Arizona singing "bomb, bomb, bomb, bomb, bomb Iran" to the Beach Boys tune of Barbara Ann, to the 2015 campaign promise of Governor Scott Walker(R) of Wisconsin, when he ran for president, promising to terminate the nuclear deal put in place by the Obama administration, to ensure Iran didn't have nuclear capabilities. Republican presidential debates in August 2015 in Cleveland, OH, said the military has two purposes, to kill and to break things. Sen. Lindsey Graham(R), from South Carolina was on the campaign trail for president from the Republican Party. He beat the drums of war vowing to "go back to Iraq and finish what we started", along with wanting war with Iran. Peace was never on the mind of this political party, and they have proved it time and again. And the basis of all of their ranting and rhetoric was based on Christianity and how they wanted to shove it down every one's throat. From illegally invading Iraq, under President George W. Bush(R), to procure their oil resources to threatening North Korea and Iran for their research into nuclear abilities. How hypocritical since the United States is the only country in the world to use nuclear weapons on another country.

The look across the lecture hall was one of amazement and disbelief. I could see the look of those who had been bred from birth to hate Iranians, and those who understood there was always another side to a coin, and actually look at it. So we talked about the current Nuclear deal negotiated with Iran.

...but, this nuclear deal was not solely brokered by the Americans and Iran. This deal took almost two years to negotiate and the other powerful countries that already possessed nuclear weapons were part of this deal. Russia, China, England, Germany and France all had input on this deal, along with the top scientist in the field of Nuclear Technology. Although it was not a perfect deal, as no negotiation is, an amicable accord was reached. Not only did these nations have input and agree to the terms, The United Nations unanimously ratified this agreement. Now to put this in perspective, the United Nations was made up of all countries that occupied this planet. So needless to say it was a pretty big deal.

One student raised his hand. He was in his late teens, early twenties, red hair cut very close and neatly to his scalp. I acknowledged him and he asked, "Do you mean to tell me Americans are responsible for what is going on?" His question was short, eloquent and direct, he deserved a response in kind. "I am merely telling you the facts. These facts are well documented and stipulated to by the CIA. The conclusion is for you to come to by researching reputable news sources, and the Agency itself." As always, I referred whenever possible, "and the Library of Congress is always a reputable source for you to do your research."
(The Republican Party and the country of Israel were the only institutions that opposed this deal, and they could not wait for the opportunity to sabotage this agreement. Unfortunately for humanity, that opportunity arose. More on that later.)

Now, no one should think of themselves important enough to ever become a target for scrutiny by their government, as long as there is no malicious intent to do irreparable harm to their government. I surely never dreamed that I would be such a target. Yes, as a tenured professor I have several published books, but there is no content in any of those writings to suggest that I had any intention of making my country or my government the focus of any mischief. The focus of all my instruction was to invoke thought in the truth and to identify the problems they incurred, witnessed or were made aware of.

Little did I know, in my State of North Carolina, that I was under such surveillance from my phone records, emails and text messages. Under the control of the right wing led faction of state government, the Governor, Pat McCrory, I was put on a watch list. Because of my more progressive and liberal train of thinking, he felt I was championing a cause for civil disobedience and supporting ISIS, a radical Islamic group that did not practice the true religion of Islam. Because by disseminating the truth, which would ultimately lead to people seeing how manipulative and deceitful the Republican party was, I was a marked man. And if you thought for yourself, you could easily research information and make educated choices when voting. No Republican currently spouting off hateful rhetoric, would ever get elected if people did their homework. So I was labeled a Domestic Terrorist by federal legislators on the right side of the aisle. Labels, even when they are false, are dangerous.

Since the governor of every state had control of the military in their states, the National Guard, they had all the technology of the United States military at their disposal. That is too much power for anyone to have that has corruption in his soul.

Not only did Governor McCrory have all my communications from the University monitored, he also had drone spy planes following me where I went throughout the state. Even when I went to do research or give a guest lecture, if it was in a Red controlled state, my activities were monitored. They networked. With thirty states out of fifty having Republican governors, their network was vast. With their ability to pry and eavesdrop, no communication was sacred. And when they wanted to monitor you, they did, without you even being aware of it. And there was no consideration to your rights when they wanted to pry.

...if you have ever traveled in the United States, it was considered relatively easy in the means of transportation you decided to use. Let us say if you wanted to drive from one end of the country to the other, you made sure your car was roadworthy, that you had enough money to put gasoline in your car to get you where your destination was, have a road map, and go. What if flying was your preference? Book a flight, pack your luggage and get on a plane, same method applied if the train was your mode of transportation.

"And we are all traveling under the suspicion of the government because of terrorism", came from a male voice from the hall. "Yeah, we never had to take our shoes off before and go through an x-ray scanner to get on a plane before, how intrusive is that?" came from another voice in the room. Slowly the tone in the room began to rise above a murmur, and I felt a full blown shouting match waiting to erupt. This is where years of experience in educating came in handy.

"Let me pose a question!", I asked in a volume that was above the audience while I still had some sense of control of my class. "If you put the pros and cons on a scale, which would outweigh which in a balancing test of the safety of pilot, crew and passengers versus the idea of unreasonable intrusiveness upon your person to board an airplane?"

As the murmurs subsided, I asked another question, "to put this to the test, who in this room feels safer knowing the person that is sitting next to you on a plane has been screened?" A consensus fell across the room, making sense that the government was working person by person to make sure no contraband to harm the plane and its passengers got onboard. The real question was, were they out thinking terrorist in ways they could possibly carry out an attack on United States soil regardless of all the technology established to ensure our security.

"Lets face it, no system is perfect, and there are ways to infiltrate and carry out a major terror attack on a major airport in this country."

Now when I made that statement, I had no idea that I was a target, and those words would get me in trouble I never wanted. "So do we want less government taking care of that problem?" I strolled across the stage that was my lecture platform, and made the argument, "In my opinion, anyone that is calling for less government is calling for a weaker country. Name one strong country in the world that has weak or limited government and I will listen to a case for less government."

When we continued the next day, the subject of September 11, 2001 by a question sparked from the audience.

...under the fear and paranoia that was created by Chicken Little crowd in the wake of the terrorist attack on the Twin Towers in New York City on September 11, 2001, the then President (or resident as I refer to him) George W. Bush, drafted a bill called, The Patriot Act. Under this law, our rights under the Fourth Amendment to our Constitution, this guaranteed all citizens the right to unreasonable search and seizure of your person, place or property you owned, without a search warrant, signed by a judge, giving government access to your privacy. The Patriot Act gave government access to this information absent a search warrant. They really screamed the "Chicken Little" nonsense! (If this were a documentary on hypocrisy of the Bush Administration, this story would go on forever! But I am trying very hard to contain my thoughts to my own story and how, by the grace of God, that those of us now here managed to escape and be free from annihilation.)

IV

…after the second Inauguration of President Obama, Republican lawmakers in Congress launched an attack on the democracy of the United States. They used tactics that resembled the Blitzkrieg of Adolph Hitler during World War II.

"Okay professor!", came a shout from the class. "Do you really want to compare Republicans to Hitler?" I laughed, shook my head reflecting a negative answer and said, "I do not want to, but the comparisons are right in front of you if you just pay attention to history."

There was no quieting the class this time. Inaudible voices rang out from the auditorium, and the looks on some of their faces were from extreme anger to those of puzzlement. I raised both my hands over my head and placed the biggest, submissive grin I could muster. "How much do you know of Hitler and his command of the media of Germany during World War II?" That was the question that brought the noise level in the class to a manageable level

…. Adolph Hitler was the ruler of Germany during World War II (WWII), and he built the most formidable armed forces in Europe. An intangible to that military might was the media. Hitler used the media, since he controlled everything, as a vehicle to dispense news slanted to the propaganda he wanted his country to believe. And the people bought it. Hitler invaded Europe, used the Italians led by Benito Mussolini, as an ally in a triad with Japan called the Axis Powers. Italy was a good ally to have because it gave Hitler direct access to the Mediterranean Sea. It also put him closer to the Suez Canal, which would have been a direct pipeline to Saudi Arabia and all the oil natural resources that Germany severely needed and lacked. Thank God the Germans lost at Cairo, or WWII would have definitely had a different outcome.

"What does that have to do with the media?"

"Where do you look for information to keep you updated on current events, the news." "How did you feel after the attack on the Twin Towers?" "What was your reaction to the shootings in Newtown, CT, or any mass shooting?" "The Paris attacks, etc…" "The reaction you feel is related to the news, how it is related to the public and the setting in which the information broadcasted."

…so what Hitler did was to use the Versailles Treaty, the event that signified World War I. The countries represented at the peace negotiations were the United States, Great Britain and France. Germany was excluded from the peace process. The effects of the Treaty left Germany in a state of depression and an economic recession. Hitler used that exclusion in the media, to justify his rise to power and the construction of one of the mightiest armies of our lifetime. He brainwashed an entire country to believe the Jews deserved to be exterminated. He brainwashed an entire country to think they were the Master Race. He convinced an entire country to go to war and eliminate those that were opposed to his Fascist government. He did this by using the media to win the minds of those that were duped into believing the bullshit he was spouting off.

"So we were all very close to speaking German!" came a yell from the audience, along with a wave of chuckles circling the room. "Much closer than you think actually." I explained Hitler's fatal flaw of bypassing the Caucasus and the vast oil resources that were there and unguarded by the Russians. Instead, Hitler chose to invade Leningrad, and the rest is history.

"Thank God Hitler was a dumbass!" came a shout from the room, and class erupted with laughter. Never let it be said Plumb was a kill joy, "I will drink to that!", I shouted back, and allowed the laughter to subside on its own.

...however in the United States, there was oil in abundance! Not only did we have enough resources to sustain ourselves, the powers that be decided to buy oil from Saudi Arabia, and stockpile it. We never lacked the resources to fuel our national defenses.

"So all we had to do was let Hitler feel the weight of the oil Russia and the United States had, and drained him of any resources he need to fight", came from a female voice in the room, one I thought sounded very familiar. I never pinpointed the source of the voice, but I had to respond. "And it is very unfortunate that it cost millions of lives before that realization came to pass", I said.

...things brings me to today's version of Hitler's media, FOX News. FOX News was that medium that Republicans used in Hitler style and fashion. They had at least three weapons they constantly used as a means of reporting; lies, misleading information and criticizing. For example, I remember watching FOX News the second day after President Obama's election in February 2009. What President Obama inherited from his predecessor, G.W. Bush, was an economy in a state of recession and depression. Millions of Americans lost money in their retirement accounts and the unemployment rate was 9.6%. FOX wasted no time blaming Obama for the state of the economy because of his "failed policies". As a rational thinking human being, I could not believe what I was hearing. How can after only two days, President Obama have had the time to implement plans that brought the economy to its knees? The answer, just one of the millions of lies and propaganda used by that news outlet. What really confuses me is how people really believed this ignorance, and could or would not process a thought to see how FOX News made stories that had no conceivable idea that was rational or based in truth.

"Did that really happen professor?" "Here is a perfect example of how you can determine for yourself the truth and see how the media on FOX News twist and distorts information." Thank goodness we live in an age of information being so fingertip ready. "Look", I said, "what was the date of President Obama's initial Inauguration?" All heads were bowed typing information on Google, Bing, or whatever internet search engine was their preference. While that was going on, I said, "Once you have that date, research FOX News during their morning news cast and see what type of criticism and news coverage he was getting on the economy."

As the jaws began to drop open one by one, and eyes grew bigger reading the text of what was being broadcast, I could hear conversations of, "he's right", and "why did my parents not tell me this stuff" start throughout the room. "Why would they make news like this if it is not true?", came out from the class. I pointed to the doors which all had a sign written in Latin, "Cogitare". That means think, which is what I always tried to inspire in my students. "Think, why would anyone want to lie to the American people?"

"To divide and conquer!" I loved the anonymity of these classroom discussions. They were free to speak, as long as it was relative and cogent to the topic of discussion. "Exactly!", I said. The only time you can have control over people is when you create a lie and make the masses think it is true. Some will believe the rhetoric, and some will see through the smoke screen. Thus you have created two or more thought processes, and divide the informed from the misinformed.

...it appears that those that tend to lean to the right were either stupid, willfully ignorant or just plain racist. The signature piece of legislation passed during President Obama's time in office was The Affordable Healthcare Act. What Republicans in Congress and the Senate did, was target that piece of legislation, and attack it with all the lies and slander they could come up with. Ted Cruz led this anti-Christian behavior, trying to deny affordable health care for all Americans. The first thing they did was to coin this law "Obama Care". This had one intention and that was to cast in a negative light on this law because of the blatant racism in Congress led by House Speaker John Boehner(R), OH. Speaker Boehner, in efforts to accomplish this, brought to the floor of the House of Representatives over fifty times that would repeal The Affordable healthcare Act, and leave millions of working Americans without access to affordable healthcare.

"It is a bad law! the government should not force anyone to have insurance." I began clapping, and said, "your argument has more merit than you think." I strolled across the floor, raised my index finger into the air and asked, "What do you propose for citizens as far as quality health care is concerned?"

I could hear thoughts across the room from reading their faces trying to come up with an answer. Finally, the only possible answer came from a female in the crowd, "Universal healthcare,a single payer system." A big grin came across my face and I was happy to reply, "Exactly!"

"Socialism is not the answer!", came from the room, and not in a very civil tone either. "Okay, time for another fact finding mission. Look to see which country has the highest rated health care system in the world?" Keyboards clicked across the room to make crickets jealous. "France!", came from the room in a loud voice. "Interesting that France has the best healthcare system in the world, anyone one know what their system is?"

More clicking, but not too much researching on this one, "France has a Democratic/Socialist Government." Again, murmurs from the class rose as if you were in a stadium and the voices of the crowd made it loud enough to hear only the person next to you. "Does anyone want to take a crack at explaining what that type of government actually looks like?" After a few seconds passed and no volunteers emerged, I told them.

...and their government is no different than ours, they elect a president, legislators and appoint their judges. The only difference is that they take care of their citizens, and their doctors do not have to worry about insurance company approvals before treating patients. That is why they are not ashamed to call themselves Socialist, because they operate under the philosophy that Socialism was intended to operate.

And this country is no different, everything that we as citizens of this country love about our nation was born out of a social program. So, if we look at Socialism for what it truly stands for, a government that takes care of its citizens rather than excluding those that are less fortunate, it has a whole new meaning.

"How can you have a Democracy and Socialism at the same time?"

"It is done all over the world in countries that elect their leaders." I went on to explain how the far right has painted a picture of negativity about the word Socialism. It was a great class, I will sum it up saying that in a free society, having health care for your citizens as a birthright is practicing the responsibilities of the Bible and the story of the "Good Samaritan". Luke 10: 29-37.

"Now, which political faction wants to end affordable healthcare for all citizens, and obstructs Universal healthcare as a right for all Americans?" After a few seconds someone yelled, "Republicans?" "Both", I said. "Remember, Hillary will not fight for that right for you, but at least there are some Democrats that want to replace the current law with a single-payer system. I challenge any of you to find a Republican politician that wants Universal Health Care. If you do, that is your man for the White House representing the Elephants."

"Yet they claim to be Christians, how hypocritical!", came from the class. "It is amazing what you can see when you open your ears." That got a big laugh, and we were done for the day.

...it is very important to understand the role of slavery in this country and how it still divides us today as a nation.

"Slavery was over one hundred fifty years ago, why do we need to talk about it?" Came from a student. "We get it, it was a bad thing now can we move on?" Reflecting on that question before answering it was the best thing I could do. I lowered my head, paced across the floor and stopped. With a big grin on my face I replied, "Well, this is a History class sir, we must cover every topic. Every bit of history, especially the bad parts because how are we supposed to learn from it if we don't even acknowledge it's existence? There might be some out there less informed than you who may want to learn something relative to current events." The class erupted and we continued. I could tell this guy did not want to look in the mirror.

...if you were unlucky enough to have been a slave in the United States, your rebellion would have been a death sentence. Yet these slave owners called themselves Christians, and believed they had the right to own people.

"I have a get to the point question professor, was the Civil War fought over slavery?" Wow, this guy cut right to the chase, I have to admit I liked it. "Indirectly, but the most important issue related to the Civil War." "Let's look through the nuts and bolts of the Civil War, then you can decide if slavery was the deciding factor in that uprising.

...if you ask anyone still sympathetic to the Confederate cause, the Civil War was fought over State's Rights. What right did those States want, slavery. They even tried legislating their own rights in opposition to Federal law called "nullification". That was the idea that the States could ignore Federal Government rules that they did not want to abide by, like slavery. So no matter how you disguise it, the Confederate States felt they had the right to own slaves, and a Civil War erupted.

"So the Civil War was fought over slavery", came a response from the class. "If it walks like a duck, quacks like a duck, etc..." "And let us not forget, these states wanting slavery have collectively referred to themselves as the Bible Belt states."

...so over this Christian idea of being able to own slaves, the United States of America was at a Civil War. So it is relevant to cover the Civil War , because it truly is the lynchpin to everything that has happened. The motto of the Confederate States was simple, the States should be able to own slaves if they wished. And if there were "less government", we could do what we want! Let the shots ring.

"Yeah, if slavery was a good Christian idea we would have a lot more than three pyramids in Egypt!" That got a laugh out of the majority of the class, and it gave me a good opportunity to pose a question. "Name one time in the history of mankind where enslaved people did not revolt?" After a few seconds, and no response, I said, "Exactly!" Man was never meant to be owned, so anyone that thinks it is their right to own another human being is no Christian, that class is what we call a racist." The class got dead silent, and I did not care. I found the urge to get biblical so I closed that topic with, "And God gave us the example that slavery is wrong which is why he sent Moses to free the Jews. Book of Exodus."

...in 1865, the Confederate States surrendered to General Ulysses Grant, and the Civil War was over, on the battlefield anyway. It is very important to remember the argument for less government was the foundation of a human right was owned by the Confederate States.

"How does this affect us today? Slavery is over and there is no threat of another Civil War."

...it affects us today because people are still maintaining that mindset of having control over others, only the methods have changed. In history we refer to owning another human being as slavery but today we call is capitalism. The idea that the Civil War is over is a fallacy. It never ended. This is typical of Washington D.C. and how our government is currently operating.

"But If we stand together we can overcome any level of racism and bigotry." I began clapping and said, "You are so right, but getting people to stand together instead of acting like it is not their problem is the issue." We began talking about the refugee crisis in the Eastern Hemisphere and how over 3800 people died by drowning in the Mediterranean Sea while trying to flee their war torn countries, but the world did not stand together. Why? Because it was not our problem, and our current lawmakers in Washington refused to help those in need. No Good Samaritan acts. I sensed a mood of despair in the room. That topic, along with discussions of the children that were washed upon shores, did nothing to bring out the Christianity of our lawmakers that claim to be so religious and run for office on the Evangelical ticket. (Good class today so far)

...it is just this man's opinion, but to me the worst thing about slavery was how the plantation master used the slaves against one another, divide and conquer if you will. Certain slaves were allowed to work in the plantation house, while the other slaves worked outside in unbearable heat and worked the fields tending to the harvest and livestock in demeaning and uninhabitable conditions. Not to mention the beatings they received at will by "Master", just because.

...these slaves that worked inside the plantation house were called "house niggers". Since they would sell out another slave to avoid working outside in subhuman conditions, this title was befitting them. Sacrificing someone else for your own benefit is the worst form of betrayal.

...since President Lincoln was a Republican, his opposition from the Bible Belt called themselves "Democrats". In the states making up this coalition, they adopted such laws that denied people of color the right to: vote, use facilities designated for "Whites Only", and to keep schools segregated. Yes, even though our Constitution said "all men are created equal", that only applied to White people. The "Dred Scott" case decided in 1857 was the model for the country at that time. The case summed up the court's opinion, and reflected the climate of the country, "even though he was a free man, he, nor any Black Man had any rights that a White man was bound to respect." This decision was written by the Supreme Court Justice, Roger Taney. You can see the mindset these Bible Belt folks and how hypocritical their actions were compared to the faith they claimed to believe in.

"I know people that still feel that way professor!" "Unfortunately, I think we all do." Class dismissed.

V

Today, I thought it necessary to fast forward to present day History. I call it that because what happened a few seconds ago, is history. Let us cover how this bigotry has carried on…

…these lawmakers on the right could not rest until they dismantled the Affordable Healthcare Act. They attacked it with lies such as the law included "death panels", poor quality of healthcare, increased premium responsibilities on the insured and overcrowding of doctors' offices.

The truth of the matter was, that the law benefitted premium holders by first off, making it affordable, hence the term "the Affordable Healthcare Act"! Do I think it is a perfect law, far from it, but to have an intelligent conversation on the topic we need to address what it does and does not do.

…the program was being paid for by the people that were buying their health insurance premiums through exchanges made available by states that allowed their tax dollars back into those states for affordable healthcare coverage. Of course the biggest states to refuse their own tax dollars back for their citizens were states that supported slavery during the United States Civil War, the Bible Belt states. Even though the law made it available, those states refused to support the law because a Black man made it law.

"Wait a minute professor, are you saying that just because Obama made this law is the only reason it is being attacked?"

"Yes." ...do not forget that the Affordable Healthcare Act was a Republican idea. Mitt Romney(R), while he was Governor of Massachusetts, enacted what we know now as "Romneycare". While he was presiding as governor of that state, he touted the law as one that should be the model for health care across the country. It is the replica of "Obama care". Take a few minutes to look it up so we can continue this discussion based in truth.

"Damn professor, they do not cover the news like this on FOX!" Those in the room that still had leanings for the right gave some pretty malicious looks, but had no comment in rebuttal. "That is why you never believe anything you hear, and learn how to get the truth on your own. That will steer you in the direction to get your source of information from, and YOU ARE RIGHT, IT WILL NOT BE FOX NEWS!"

...over eight million citizens have been able to get health insurance because of this law. But so many more would have but not for this racial hatred that still exists in this country. Only thirty six states have adopted expanding medicare coverage under the law. That leaves fourteen states that are refusing the tax dollars back into their states for medical coverage for those taxpayers. "Why?"

"Because no one wants insurance forced upon them." I raised my finger and shouted, "Eureka!" No one expected that response from me. "Feels like too much Government, right?"

"Yeah", came from the same crowd that had no response to the Romney research. "Just by a show of hands, who thinks mandatory car insurance is ok if you own a car?" About ninety nine percent of hands went up in the room. "And who can tell me which President made auto insurance mandatory?" After a few minutes of keyboard clicking a student replied, "Reagan(R)". I nodded my head an affirmation and asked, "So if I understand all of you, you think it is more important to protect a car and not a person?" I waited, but silence drowned the atmosphere. No response.

...is the analogy any clearer now. When it was Romney proclaiming the law it was fine. But because Obama did it that was unacceptable. So when Romney ran for President under the platform of repealing the Affordable healthcare Act, his own idea, racism is the only conclusion I can come up with. "That is why I did not support Romney in his campaign for the Presidency, he showed he was a puppet to his biggest donors, the Koch brothers. Which stands to reason he was not going to represent me, or any of you in here.

"But Obama is not representing us either!" I heard lots of agreement on that one, and I asked, "How is he not representing you?, and I do not want to hear stereotypes,or general trash talking without supporting facts." "Well like you said professor, his health care law is incomplete." I nodded my head and said, "That is true sir, but the intent of the law is what, to give more people access to that health care that was not available to them before. How is that not representing people like you?" It was time to debunk the lies spread by Republican lawmakers and their donors, the Insurance Industry, not to mention the vehicle they used, FOX News.

...so everyone, go to the Library of Congress website, and search for "Obama care". the keyboards clicked away, and when many of them waited further instruction, I asked, "Does everyone have the Bill in front of them?" When enough of them, for my satisfaction, nodded affirmative, I said, "research the section where you can stay on your parent's insurance til you are 26." He walked right into a haymaker with that question really, this guy was proof that he hated the President based on rhetoric instead of fact.

...everyone of you in this this room is represented by this law. Prior to the Affordable Healthcare Act being passed, all of you in here would not have health insurance because you are adults. If anything were to happen to you today, you can go to the doctor because mommy and daddy still get to pay for you til you are twenty six years of age. Before this law, you would be on your own. So I ask, are you being represented by this law? Which one of you in here is offended you can still go to the doctor while someone else pays for it? Again, dead silence in the room.

...the law removed caps that insurance companies paid so they could no longer deny paying claims for people that seriously needed their medicine and medical treatments. Does that not represent you?

...the law restricted how much health insurance companies could pay for advertising, and if they exceeded that amount they had to refund a portion of insurance premiums to its policyholders. On a side note, my premiums were reduced as a result of this law. The amount I paid to have my wife and daughter on my plan was reduced by half. Do not tell me the law was necessary, it worked and was a positive thing for the American people. I can say it represented me. And now I believe every one of you in here can say it has represented you as well.

...I will share a little piece of my personal life to you. One of my oldest and dearest friends in the world is a conservative, and he means well. We were having a conversation one day, and he said he likes to listen to conservative media. Class, that is exactly the problem. He and conservatives like him only want to hear what they want to hear. That is why they watch FOX News, and listen to people on the far right trying to pull America down like Rush Limbaugh, Glen Beck, Ann Coulter. Those media outlets only broadcast news from that point of view. They label any other source of media like National Public Radio, as Liberal media, spouting off leftist information. The truth of the matter is, those sources of media do not broadcast news from a Liberal point of view, they are unbiased and reporting the facts from the ground source. That is why it is so important to me that when we view history, we look at it from the perspective of the truth rather than what spin you try and label it with.

...but Republican lawmakers in Congress and the Senate were so intent on destroying this law, they, led by Sen. Ted Cruz(R), from Texas, led the charge to shut down the government over it. So, Speaker Boehner refused to pay the country's bills, i.e. Obamacare, and they let the government shutdown for eighteen days and threatened to default on the government's obligations. This was a game of flinch, and the Elephants thought Obama would flinch first. He did not, and at the last minute an agreement was reached to fund the government.

"After you look at it like from the point of view that these guys wanted to take something away from us, Republicans in Congress and Ted Cruz look like assholes", popped of a student. I laughed and repeated, "If it walks like a duck…"

"I am not voting Republican this next election". That sentiment started to reverberate throughout the class. I have to admit, it felt good watching them make the connection of who is responsible for the gridlock in Washington D.C.

…but let's look at HR Bill 2775 that reopened the government. There were 19 senators that voted "nay", keep the government shutdown. Ted Cruz was one of those Senators. He is also running for President of the United States on the Republican ticket. Of course he is still beating the drums to repeal the law that still gives you access to health care. On a side note, he also wants to renege on the nuclear deal with Iran and send the United States back to war. Does that sound like he is representing any of you?
Another good class.

…who can tell me what minimum wage means? From the audience came the nonsense the right keeps feeding America's, "Minimum Wage is for minimal skilled jobs." That was exactly the answer I thought I would hear.

...in my travels throughout the vastness that was the world, one thing is irrefutable, no man wants to be taken care of! This myth that minorities were lazy and being labeled as "takers" could not be farther from the truth. Last count, the average household that received food stamps, a government run program to help families put food on the table, got roughly $130 per month. It was written in the law that these vouchers could only be used for food items. It was impossible to ring up things like cigarettes, alcohol or non-edible items with system. Yet Republicans beat the drum of "moochers" using their tax dollars to live the so called "Life of Riley", meaning you had an easy and comfortable life for nothing in return. A welfare king and queen.

...the truth of the matter was, that millions of Americans that received government assistance were working multiple jobs to try and make ends meet yet still needed help just to eat. FOX News broadcasted these lies about the "takers" as if they were leaches on society. This message was broadcast daily, to inspire voters to vote Republican and eliminate the system set in place to help those less fortunate.

I put my own copy of the Minimum Wage law on the wall behind me.

...in 1938, federal legislators created a standard, or minimum wage, for all non-supervisory employees. The legislative intent of this law was to establish the minimum needed to sustain a living. It was written into the text of the bill that was enacted. The oohs and ahs drummed through the class when I put that part of the legislative text on the wall. "Nowhere in the law is it defined that minimum wage is for minimal skilled jobs."

...but Congress never implemented a plan to factor in cost of living expenses and how they grew exponentially. President Bill Clinton (D) from 1992-2000, was the last president to increase the minimum wage in the United States to the whopping sum of $7.25 per hour. That increase marked the last time congress did anything for the millions of working Americans that lived in the United States.

...you see, the Massachusetts Institute of Technology (MIT), one of the most prestigious institutions of higher learning, conducted a study in 2013, on the issue of minimum wage. They concluded that if the minimum wage would have kept pace with inflation, that wage would have been $20.74 per hour. But what the right have been saying are the lies of what the law really is. That for decades now, was that minimum wage was for minimal skill positions. They all stared at me like i was giving free candy away. The light went on how the rich have manipulated the public, by conservative media broadcasting these lies for their own profit.

...the fatal flaw in this line of thinking is that first of all it was not true. Secondly, the reasonable man would conclude minimal skilled jobs should equate to minimal skilled profits. The stage was mine, no comments from the peanut gallery, the light had exposed the lies the right had been saying solely for the purpose of higher profits.

...except the majority of these companies and organizations made billions of dollars per year in profit off the work of the so called minimal skilled labor positions. In my opinion, it models the plantation style model of business and to get rich off the fruit of others work.

Finally a nerve had been struck, "so the fast food industry like McDonald's, and places like Walmart are the problem?" The answer is much deeper than that, so I thought carefully for a second before answering. "Yes, but it is important to understand the nuts and bolts of why".

...industries like this spend lots of money paying our lawmakers to continue making legislation that allows them to pay less taxes, if any, keep the minimum wage as low as possible, and not have to pay any benefits because the grunt force of their operation is at part-time.

"The fast food industry operates on a franchise owner basis, so the corporations themselves do not own the restaurants, right?" This was another light to shine on this topic. "Class, pick any fast food franchise and see how much it cost to buy one." The research began and the eyes in the room grew to optimal potential as they looked at some of the prices for the privilege of owning one of these businesses.

"McDonald's requires at least a $300,000 deposit if you do not have the full amount. they will not even say what the full amount is." The room let out a concurrent audible of "damn", and "Shit". along with other expletives I do not need to mention. "And do any of you have $300,000 to give to someone for the privilege of selling heart attacks a Happy Meal at a time?" No silver spoons in this class I guess because no one raised their hands or replied aloud in the affirmative. "So pretty much you have to be in the class of the "haves" to be in a position to even own a fast food franchise." That hammer nailed the coffin shut.

...since greed was at the top of the list for employers, part-time employees were the preferred hire. So if you were fortunate enough to work full-time, that $7.25 equaled little over $15,000 per year. "Does anyone in this room think that is enough to live on?"

...now this should give a clear picture as to how the rich continued to get rich off the labor of the poor and expendable.

...the employees that work in this industry are the class of people that needed subsidies from the government at about an average of $130 of food on the table. These were the people labeled "takers". These were the people that made America habitable, and these were the people that were considered a dark spot on the country. These people are the bygone middle class.

...I remember making this argument at the graduating class of law school students at Duke one year, the event that kickstarted the path that put me on the run for my life, because the Dean felt a historical perspective to the next group of lawmakers, was a good idea. Well, I kind of had enough went out to left field and spoke on the idea of "makers vs takers". I proposed a series of questions to the class, "do you know how many days of the year congress and the senate actually spend in session? Do you know how much a current sitting congressman or senator makes? Lastly, do you know how much an ex-congressman or ex-senator makes? The youngest and brightest minds looked at me through eyes of bewilderment. These were simple questions, answers that were easily accessible if you just looked for the information. 130 days a year is the average that our legislators worked, made over $100,000 per year, and this is if you were currently serving or just used to. I ask anyone that may read this, have any of you ever worked 130 days a year and made that kind of money? Stupid question, never mind. Who really sounds like the takers? As a nation, we have the right to change laws were unnecessary spending of taxpayer dollars should be spent. I argue that anyone that made over $100,000 per year and only worked 130+ days a year should be subject to term limits. It would only make sense then that anyone, after leaving office should also be relieved of retirement and health care for life at taxpayer expense. This would save much more taxpayer dollars than attacking the working family that received $130 per month, at least the working man and woman actually produced and provided for the needs of the people.

...remember, working harder makes the company you worked for richer, not you. So that argument made no sense in the reality of the mom or dad to put more stress on them to always do more. You were either paid by the hour or a paid salary employee. Only those in the "in crowd" had the positions that received bonuses, and that was all made off the backs of the employees told to "work harder". The joke was on them in the long run, I hated giving speeches more than they ever .wanted me to give another one! Lol, I just hope it made reasonable sense to a young ambitious type who wanted to legislate for the people instead of the wealthy that lined their pockets to pass laws for the rich. It never stopped me from writing though.

That gave everyone in the room a laugh, and we ended on a high note.

The next "think tank" would be an interesting one. I gave a simple investigative assignment;

1. Pick any currently sitting United States Congressman
2. What voting district do they serve
3. How long have they been in office
4. Who are their campaign contributors

5. List every bill they have ever voted on, or abstained from

6. How did that vote affect their voting constituents and the rest of the country

Pretty simple assignment, or so I thought. Knowing that some students strive to be as lazy as possible I assumed I would have duplicate, maybe triplicate congressmen/women if they have been in office a relatively short period of time, it would be interesting to see what each student discovered and from what point of view they would look at the information from.

Rep. Markwayne Mullin(R) of Oklahoma would do. He was a very good example actually.

...his tenure in Congress has been relatively short, yet the Second District of Oklahoma has experienced a significant number of natural disaster possibilities, with the number of increased earthquakes in that region of the country. That number is so significant, because the average amount of tremors in eastern Oklahoma have risen from two, to over five thousand. How is this Rep. Mullin's responsibility you may ask, and the answer is "fracking". Hydraulic fracking, or fracturing of the Earth's mantle, is the method used to extract natural gas from under our feet. Natural gas is supposed to be a cleaner burning fuel, but the negatives of the fracking process far outweigh the positives gained by utilizing this method. To really understand how ecologically dangerous this is, all you had to do was watch the movies "Gasland" or "Gasland II" . Those documentaries explained the criminality of this process and the greedy people that promote fracking.

...Congressman Mullin supported this action, by receiving more money than you or I would ever see, from the Oil and Gas Industry, the Koch Brothers, Insurance industry, and any other very wealthy person to go to Congress and ruin the land his voting constituents live on. That is a prime example of people voting against their own best interest. A true Representative, Democrat or Republican, that does not take money from Super PAC'S,and believes we need to act immediately on the issue of Climate Change, is the right person for that job, not you Mr. Mullin.

...let us broaden our scope on the entire State of Oklahoma, a Bible Belt state. I will not go into a history lesson on Oklahoma, just the relevant parts that pertain to the issue of fracking in that state. It will not take long either. The majority State Legislative body is predominantly Republican. The Governor, State House Speaker, State Senate leader are all Republican. Republicans control how laws are made in that Bible Belt state. Period. But look for yourself, you will always do better looking at the information yourself rather than blindly believing anyone.

A few keyboards clicked, but the obvious is obvious, and we continued.

...the top scientist in the field of the geographical studies proved that fracking was determined to be the direct cause of the substantial amount of earthquakes the state has been victim to. Oklahoma lawmakers enacted legislation forbidding the restriction or halting of fracking in that state. If people payed attention, Republicans would not be in control of legislation in Oklahoma. Prime example of believing the lies broadcasted on FOX News about denying severe climate change exist, and voting Republican, against your own best interest.

VI

...getting people to do what is against their own best interest is the key to victory, divide and conquer, use any analogy you like, that is what tactics the right stood for. Conjuring and fabricating falsehoods, and using the "Chicken Little" playbook to stir up fear among the masses is easy when you have access to global television networks, newspaper and radio tools to reach the masses.

...unfortunately, those people do not check the source of information they receive, and the people are scared into thinking one thing or source of terror is the reason for what is wrong. The truth is, FOX News is criminally negligent as being the major contributor to this paranoia. Until they see the truth for what it is, fear will always be a good tool to stir up the masses into the frenzy you have created, and thus are led to slaughter. Foxy Loxy wins. Coincidentally, FOX News bears the same name as that conniving predator from our children's story.

"So that is why you always challenge us to search the truth instead of just listening to you." "Exactly!", I replied, "once you leave this class and enter the working and contributing to our society class, you will have to stay truthfully informed. You will have to educate your children, should you choose to have any. Most importantly, you will have the power to vote and elect people into office that will actually represent the people and not big money or the insane."

...but if you disagree with the right, nothing good would happen to you. They acted like the kid in the schoolyard who took his ball and went home because the game was not going his way. Evidence: Republicans when President Bill Clinton(D) was in the White House. Ken Starr wasted over $40 million dollars of taxpayer money investigating the Clinton's to find nothing. Notwithstanding how they repeated the same behavior Wasting taxpayer dollars on bogus claims that also revealed nothing. It is either their way or we are going to block and obstruct everything we can, Boo Hoo. Bunch of cry babies i my opinion.

"Yeah!", came from the audience, "Now that Paul Ryan(R) is Speaker of the House, he just brought a bill to the floor to repeal Obamacare again, you are right!" This girl pays attention I said to myself. "And now that Republicans have control of the Senate, a bill was passed there as well to repeal the Affordable Healthcare Act. They will stop at nothing." I raised my hand to signal I was not finished. I walked back to my podium, and went to my internet search engine. "Our Senate majority leader, Mitch McConnell(R) is on record saying he will do nothing to support our President". I played soundbites of Sen. McConnell admitting to this allegation, along with clips of him after President Obama's initial Inauguration saying he would do everything in his power to ensure he was a one term president.

"And look at all those Crackers in the picture with him, all wanting to go back to Segregation!" I could not deny I felt the same way as that student, but in order to get past this era of hatred based on skin color, I had to address that comment. "That type of descriptive language is what is perpetrating the continuing divide of Americans that agree with you. Please use adjectives that are less inflammatory while in class. Maybe the term "White Men" would be less offensive and still be totally accurate."

...needless to say, these "White Men", (laughter) were definitely the ones not representing you. Being poor, and not getting proper health care as a result of it,rather it be from not having health insurance or not being able to afford to use it because of co-pays and deductibles, and voting Republican is voting against your own best interest.

"Amen professor!" And Class was done for the day.

This semester had been going so well in terms of discussion, fact finding, and the understanding of knowledge is power, that I decided today to let the discussion flow where it wanted to go. To start things off, I thought a trip into segregation was in order, because I hoped the conversation would flow toward an epiphany of one basic thing, how to vote in your own best interest. "How did this country become so politically divided?" I paced the floor waiting for an intelligent response. I did not wait too long, after fifteen seconds or so I said, "would you believe me if I told you it was over the Right to Vote?" Some murmurs rose, but not many, "because it is true, let us reflect, then you can surmise what can be done to remedy this divide."

...I think it is best to start with the landmark case of Brown vs. Board of Education. Even though it does not address the issue of voting, it clearly displays the attitudes of those advocating segregation and the basic rights of the people in this country.

...this case hinged on the question is, was separate considered equal in the eyes of the law regarding the level and quality of education between Black and White students. Once again the calls for less government started, and White citizens of the Bible Belt began displaying the Confederate Flag. The flag of the Confederate Army during the Civil War. That symbol, the "Stars and Bars", that represented another country and declared war on the United States over their Christian belief of slavery.

"Slavery is not a Christian belief", came from the class. "Very true, however, remember the group of people that wanted slavery were in the self proclaimed Bible Belt states. I say that with the most amount of sarcasm as possible when I say those things."

...once again, that flag began flying again as a symbol that they still believed in, segregation. That was just the way of the south. It was right here in the south that these "Jim Crow" laws existed making segregation legal in the first place. That flag flew on state property in the Bible Belt, proof that they had no intentions of ever treating fairly or equally, people of color. They did not want government telling them they had to integrate their schools, and the song of "less government" rang out once again in these Bible Belt states.

"He is right again, just read the Constitution of the Confederate States." So much information out there I thought to myself, I am glad this student had the initiative to continue making sure this discussion was based in truth.

...once again, look where the rally cry began for this theme. The theme of racial inequality. You know, I never understood how anyone could think of themselves superior over another human being based solely on the color of one's skin. Sound like the Civil War was over in the minds of the Bible Belt? Apparently not.

...I digress to my elementary school days for a demonstration of why it is never good to judge another based on physical differences. When I was in third grade, the United States had just signed the Civil Rights Law into law. As a result of this, our educational system performed an experiment to bring home the point of prejudices, and why it was wrong to practice that way of thinking.

Our class was separated into blue eyed students and brown eyed students. As if segregating the class did not feel comfortable enough from the start, the blue eyed students were told they were superior to the brown eyed students, therefore they were allowed to line up first for recess and lunch, they did not have to participate in cleaning the class at the end of the day and were first to line up to go home at the end of the day. Needless to say, some friendships were strained by the end of the school day. The following day, the blue eyed students came to school continuing their exhibitions of superiority and entitlement privileges they had the previous day. To their chagrin, our teacher changed to rules and gave all the privileges from the previous day to the brown eyed students. The blue eyed students showed feeling of regret for their behavior, and begged the brown eyed students for forgiveness and help with all the classroom responsibilities. Even though we wanted to end the simulation, our teacher made the blue eyed students finish their obligations so they would get the full benefit of the exercise. We were a more closely knit class after that experience. I loved the benefit of an educational system that taught tolerance and acceptance.

...even though the Supreme Court ruled that "separate was not equal", and that the practice of segregation in public schools was illegal, this did not deter the blind hatred that White people had against people of color. Gangs, like the Ku Klux Klan practiced acts of terrorism in violent and destructive means by burning crosses on properties that were owned by Black people. Churches where people of color worshiped were defamed in this fashion by cross burnings, painting inflammatory comments and insignias like swastikas, the symbol of Hitler's Nazi Party during WWII. Most heinously of all, these places of worship, houses of God, were bombed and burned to the ground, many times while people were in church doing nothing but praying. And you guessed it, these Klan members were in church every Sunday, worshiping to the god that believed in violence and hatred. You gotta love the Bible Belt!

"I think all of us should have participated in that exercise as children!" That sentiment was received with such class approval, it sounded like of wave of "Yeah" going across the room. "Maybe some of you will go into Education as a pathway to your career. Feel free to use this to start a ripple of tolerance and not hatred."

...here is where things really went downhill. Prior to 1965, Black people in the United States did not have the universal right to vote. Once again, it was the states in the Bible Belt that was denying people of color from voting. These White, so called Christians, would not only make threats of violence on Black people if they tried to vote, lynchings were a common practice, and no one was ever prosecuted for murders like this. Local law enforcement doubled as Klansmen in their off duty time, a well as judges and just plain hateful people. And after all, who is going to miss a nigger? Forgive me for using that term as I truly despise it and the origin from whence it came.

...yet this was the value placed on Black lives by White people. Lynching was a practice in the United States by White people that never died. And no one was ever prosecuted for these crimes. It is easy to formulate the conclusion that these Bible Belt states could easily have been monikered as "the non-Bible Belt states."

...naturally, it was those so called Christians in the Bible Belt states crying like little school girls because they had to now permit Black people to vote. Less government cries rang out once more because if those states did not want people of color to vote then the government should not force them to allow it. I hope by now you have seen when the battle cry for less government ripples through the country its roots can be traced directly to racial hatred.

"You make it hard to refute that claim professor. I know too many people in my neighborhood that still think that way." Unfortunately, I did too.

...when President Johnson signed the Civil Rights Bill into law, he was quoted as saying, "this law just cost Democrats the White House". This was the time that the Democrats in the Bible belt states declared allegiance for the Republican Party, all over "less government", because the law of the land was that now people of color could vote. As usual, their version of christianity was, if they did not want Black people to vote, then government should not force them to let Black people vote. Funny how christianity in the Bible Belt states meant Black people were not worthy of voting.

..now here is where the great political divide occurred in this country.

...the next Presidential election, the race for the White House was divided in a three way battle. Vice President Hubert Humphrey(D), Richard Nixon(R) and George Wallace(I). George Wallace at the time was Governor of the State of Alabama, a Bible Belt state. He was actually a Democrat, but ran on the Independent ticket due to Vice President Humphrey getting the nomination from the Democratic Party.
Wallace was a vocal advocate for "segregation", keeping Blacks out of White schools. Thus, the Black Colleges of this country were formed from this segregation.

...contrary to the propaganda disseminated on FOX News, Black Colleges were formed out of necessity because they were not permitted in White Schools. Not because of the lie that Black Colleges were formed to keep White people out. So Gov. Wallace was definitely promoting the separatist, racist, agenda by running on that theory would land him the Presidency. Kind of how the candidates on the Republican ticket are thinking by their inflammatory rhetoric.

"History keeps repeating itself, huh professor?", came from the crowd. "That is because too many of us are not interested in keeping ourselves informed." And that is a sad truth.

...Vice President Humphrey lost a narrow decision to Nixon, and the south has been Republican ever since, all because of the right to let Black people vote. These were the people yearning for a government ruled on "Christian" values. These were the people that wanted to proudly display the emblem of the Confederate States. These were the people that wanted less government in their lives so they could still be free to practice the open hatred and racism they wanted. These were the people screaming "Free Barabbas!" These were the people that do not want to be PC (politically correct) because they want to be able

...now that the Republicans had control of the Bible Belt states, let us never forget how they got that control. Let us never forget how they used suppressive and discriminatory practices to maintain that control.

...we have covered the Affordable healthcare Act as it relates to you. How has it represented other Americans? let us take a look. I put a list of benefits on the screen behind me, and showed how its intent was help everyone.

"So why is it that all we hear are bad things about the law when everything you show us puts Obama care in a bad light?" I really did not want to beat a dead horse regarding the media, so I changed the screen to show everything that president Obama accomplished in his tenure as our President:

1.The Affordable Healthcare Act-gave millions of working Americans access to quality and affordable healthcare

2. Over 200,000 jobs created in private job sector growth since the inception of the Affordable Healthcare Act

3. Continued growth in the economy by 2.5% since the inception of the Affordable Healthcare Act

4. Unemployment dropped during his presidency, from 9.6% when he took office from his predecessor, to 5%

5. Production of energy from renewable sources increased by 33%, reducing the flow of carbon emissions into the atmosphere

6. Allowed over eleven million people that were currently in the United States but born in other countries to legally remain in the United States. (These people were referred to as "illegal immigrants")

…but most of all, President Obama accomplished something that no other President has been able to accomplish, he had face to face, diplomatic, negotiations with the Nation of Iran, to ensure Iran would not obtain a nuclear weapon. The only rhetoric you hear coming from the right was war, war, war.

…for upcoming presidential elections held in November 2016, there were seventeen candidates running on the Republican ticket. Some of the outlandish, moronic, immature and discriminatory rhetoric was being used by every one of these candidates.

...no one had any rights they were concerned about, not people of color, people of the gay and lesbian communities, people with disabilities, women and immigrants from other countries. Predominantly anywhere from the Middle East to the country of Mexico.

"They should stay in their own countries and leave us alone." Some people just do not get it, "With that line of thinking sir, you should be living in Europe." That made the class erupt with oohs and ahhs.

...the ideas that Donald Trump espoused were to not only build a wall dividing and segregating the United States from Mexico, he vowed to have the country of Mexico pay for it, because the people that they send over here are criminals,drug dealers and rapist. He stereotyped all people of the Muslim faith of being terrorist and they should not be allowed in the United States.

I had one point to make, "To be honest,every Muslim I have ever encountered in my life has been a person of peace, goodwill and healthy lifestyles. Muhammad Ali, Heavyweight Champion of the world, was stripped of his title because he refused to fight in Vietnam. Sounds peaceful to me, and he has always been an Ambassador of Peace, preaching to the world that violence is never the answer.

...pay attention to all the candidates as if you have never met them, and listen to what they have to say. "Would any of you stand behind breaking up families? Cutting wages? Denying health care as a right?" I had their attention because no one would want that for themselves, "Then why would you support anyone that does?"

...now look at who is spouting off things like "it's not my problem", and acting like "you are a loser" because you were not born with a "silver spoon" up your ass like Trump was, and Jeb. All line of thinking in that direction is coming from one place, the Republican Party.

"Who do you support for President professor?"

Thinking along the thought process of steering them to think for themselves and not being persuaded to vote for, I said, "I support the candidate that will increase the minimum wage and attach it to the rate of inflation. I support the candidate that will provide healthcare to every American as a birthright. I support the candidate that is committed to getting this country on course to being one hundred percent powered on green energy." (Those were the things I was most concerned about)

...here is a story that might interest you. In my opinion, this is the definition of hypocrisy, and evidence of my disdain for the right

...Arkansas State legislator, Josh Miller(R), is in a wheelchair. He was a huge supporter of NOT expanding the Affordable Healthcare Act for the citizens of that state, and yes, it was a Bible Belt state, suprised? Even though he was guaranteed free healthcare for the rest of his life, provided by the taxpayers of the United States, he cast his support in efforts to deny it to anyone else. Thank god this hypocrite was not running for President, but he sure supported anyone that Republicans nominated.

"Damn professor, preach!"

...returning to the issue of Trump, I remember when he went to Phoenix, in the State of Arizona. To fully cast a light on how Republicans were and how hateful they were,Ii was actually at a rally for a Democratic candidate, Bernie Sanders(I) from Vermont. The mood and atmosphere at this rally was very different than the Trump rally. At the Trump rally, protesters were out in force, showing solidarity for their support against him and his racist comments about the Mexican people. Police were present to ensure no violence erupted, which none did, and Trump supporters were yelling some of the most hateful, racist, and derogatory language with such animosity displayed on their White faces. It characterized that crowd as malicious and venomous in nature, just calling it as it happened.

...turns out at the Sanders rally, the mood was polarized from that of the Trump crowd. There were no police present, the crowd, over 11,000 to Trump's 5000, was very peaceful. It was a very diverse crowd too, there were many retirees, women, people of all nationalities, young middle aged, gay and lesbian and those that attended gave the evening a pleasant and welcoming feeling. It felt like there was hope of living in a society of where people from all walks of life could live together, realizing that we were are all God's children and should welcome one another and accept their offerings they have from the cultures and experiences they posses so we could all benefit from gifts we were given instead of feeling like it was every man for himself. (Alas, it came down to every man for himself, and it did not have to be this way

...another one of Trump's brilliant and humane campaign promises, of course i am kidding you, was to not only rescind President Obama's Executive Order, allowing over 11,000,000 undocumented immigrants legal access to being the United States, but to take it a step farther. Trump had the audacity to suggest that any person born in the United States from parents that were here undocumented (illegally), would be deported along with their parents. Let me just say, as a Christian man, I am extremely offended by the term "illegal alien" or "immigrant". Jesus Christ, the son of God, never taught to build a wall bordering your neighboring country, or anyone you felt did not belong where you were. In the Bible, in the Book of Joshua, God tells Joshua how to bring the walls of Jericho down so the Jews could enter the promised land. But you go ahead and build your wall Mr. Trump, you are one of the people who does not learn their lesson unless it is the hard way. Even the Great Wall of China could not keep the Huns out

"You were at both rallies professor?" She seemed surprised I would attend a Republican rally. "How else would I be able to actually give you information with which to compare?" And I believed that. Television does not truly capture the tension in the atmosphere because you will not get struck by a projectile from your living room. I actually spoke with a reporter from the Arizona New Times magazine while I was at the Sanders rally. She told me she was not allowed inside the Trump rally even though she was Press. Trump only wants supporters, he can not handle any criticism she was telling me.

...pay attention to the news, not FOX,(that got a chuckle) these guys running on the side of the Elephants were being as exclusive and fearful as ever. They cheered at FOX News, as they listened to the ideas Trump was spewing from his mouth about "anchor babies".

"I do not get it, what does that term mean?", came from a female student. "It means the mother and father are "anchored" to the United States now because their child was born here making that child a citizen of this country."

...the only problem with that argument was that it was a guaranteed right by the 14th Amendment to the Constitution that any person born in the United States shall be considered a citizen of this country. So Trump, who called these people "anchor babies", (what an offensive term) was on his high horse actually promising to deport American citizens, and the racist were there every step of the way, cheering at FOX News that would be on in public places such as, bars, barber shops, airport terminals, doctor office waiting rooms, the gym, dentist, appliance stores, etc…

...the more unbiased news channels, like MSNBC, or AL-JAZEERA America, were never on in such places. This is a true story. One time I was at the gym and I was on a cardiovascular exercise piece of equipment watching AL-JAZEERA. Some guy came in and started yelling, I kid you not, because he was not going to watch that crap, as he put it, on the television. He refused to keep his voice down, would not respect that I was watching that segment and the story was pretty good. There was a new advancement in solar technology, which I could not wait to share with Jack, and it was capable of storing more solar energy which would help reduce carbon emissions and save homeowners money on energy cost. He would not listen, and heaven forbid actually learn something, he just kept trying to talk louder than the television and proclaiming how much of a fucking asshole he was.

"Where was this professor?", came from the room. "I was in Arkansas."

...and yes, that is a Bible Belt state. In my opinion, how myopic. The refusal to expand their minds and try to hear what is being said rather than acting childish just because of the channel that the television was on. His rationale was that AL-jazeera was showing Muslims cheering after the attacks of September 11. I told him that using that logic we would never watch FOX News again because they showed it too. It was fun getting his goat after a while.

"Pretty funny professor."

...there was no room for absorbing any rational thought on the part of Republicans. I could always tell when i was at a difference of opinion with someone, they would go into what I called "parrot mode" and just keep repeating the same rhetoric without offering any cogent thought or reason to the conversation. I knew I had them, so I would let them just go on making themselves look stupid. It was too easy.Do not think that Trump is exclusive to this train of thought among Republican Presidential candidates

....Sen. Ted Cruz(R) from the State of Texas, a Bible Belt state, expressed a similar point of view. Texas was a border state along the Mexican boundary to the United States. This is the state where President John Kennedy(D) was assassinated, no coincidence he was a strong advocate for civil and human rights in the United States. This was the state where President Lyndon Johnson(D) was from, and a United States Senator prior to becoming Kennedy's Vice President. This is the state that began the movement to switch to the Republican Party after Johnson signed the Civil Rights Bill into law.

This state was at its core, racist. Here is where Cruz' hypocrisy is displayed. Cruz himself was born in the country of Canada, by our Constitution, he was ineligible to run for President because he was not born in the United States, as was required by law. But through a loophole, he was allowed to put his hat in the ring.

...Ted Cruz' father was born in Cuba, a country Republicans wanted to eradicate off the face of the map,because their leader, Fidel Castro. He was a Communist, and allied Cuba with Russia, the most powerful Communist country in the world. Cruz' mother however, was a United States citizen, so he could declare himself a "naturalized citizen" and be eligible to run for President as a United States citizen. The only hurdle in his way was denouncing formally, that he was abdicating any right to his Canadian citizenship, which he gladly did. This guy is at the heart of the cancer that was the Republican Party.

"Why do you say that professor?" I explained how he went nationwide preaching how bad a law this was. He blatantly lied to the American people about the law ignoring all the benefits we have covered during this semester. And worst of all, he led the charge the shut the government down over the Affordable Healthcare Act. The law that gave you the right to have health care while you are sitting in this room.

...so naturally, to reward Republicans for shutting down the government over trying to deny healthcare to American citizens, in November 2014, Americans elected Republicans to a majority of the Senate. Even after the second time the Supreme Court deemed the Affordable Healthcare Act constitutional, Republicans continued their vow to dismantle the law. Does this make sense to anyone? Again, this did not have to happen, more on that later, hopefully. Let me get back to immigration.

...other Republican candidates latched onto this term of "anchor baby", spitting out such venomous lies like, women of the Mexican persuasion were waiting at the border in their last trimester, then coming across the border to have their child so he/she would be an American citizen. Jeb Bush(R) one such candidate, took it a step further and accused the Asian population of being the biggest contributor to this problem. I already was not a supporter of his candidacy because of how he used government in the most intrusive manner involving a husband and wife. All i have to say is "Terry Schiavo", and Fuck You Jeb! You were such a hypocrite, it made me barf to look at you, and your brother George, President Obama's predecessor. The pain and suffering you caused the American people for your own benefit and blaming it on the only Black President this country ever had, is what showed me the Devil lived in the White House for eight years during YOUR brother's Presidency.

...I substantiate this by starting this on the war George W. Bush initiated against the country of Iraq and its leader, Saddam Hussein. But again, let me get back to the issue of immigration, the war in Iraq deserves its own conversation. For certainty, Jeb Bush was not in favor of immigration reform nor a pathway to citizenship for immigrants wanting to come to the United States.

...in my opinion the biggest joke among these candidates was Louisiana Governor, Bobby Jindal(R). His birth parents were born in the country of India, which makes this so funny. Jindal jumped on the bandwagon of "anchor babies", and for deporting children born from undocumented parents. Well Governor, sounds pretty hypocritical since you fell into that catagory yourself! With that line of thinking you disqualified yourself from being President, you were truly a mental midget. But let us not stop there, remember the self portrait you had done making yourself more of a tan colored person rather than your true coffee colored skin. It was very evident to me how badly you wished you were White, and how little self esteem you had since you did not hesitate to suck the White man's dick for money to keep legislation in place that benefited the rich and fuck the little guy over. Prime example, you refused to accept tax dollars back into Louisiana, that the taxpayers paid, to provide affordable healthcare for the citizens in your state. You would rather get on your knees before the Koch brothers, one of the largest donors to the Republican Party, for money rather than take care of the citizens of Louisiana. Your strive to be White other than accept your family heritage and be proud of where your family came from, another country under White rule, the British Empire, you adopted the "house nigger" philosophy for yourself and that is why you never got my support.

...once again, lawmakers felt that they could forget ignore that the United States was founded on immigration. From the inception of this country, the motto for how we treat those that came there in search of a better life for their families and the chance of making something of yourself and for yourself. That motto and creed for this belief was engraved on the Statue of Liberty, which read: "Give me your tired, your poor, your huddled masses yearning to breathe free".

...nowhere on that plaque did it say, "unless you are Mexican or Muslim". Nowhere in the Bible did it say to turn your back on your neighbor and treat him unwelcomingly. And, nowhere in the Bible did it say to stay on your side of the line. Instead, it gave us a commandment to love one another the way he loved us.

...you will never find an example of Jesus Christ treating anyone with disdain and contempt. But you will find countless examples of Republican legislators acting and preaching that very hatred. Whether it be in church every sunday and calling themselves christians or judging others for lifestyles that were different from theirs, those people were labeled terrorist, un-American or un-Christian. I believe if Jesus Christ were on the face of this earth today, he would call everyone preaching how devoute their faith is, a Pharisee. They were all hypocrites in my opinion. And these were the people responsible for creating the diplomatic relations between The United States, Mexico and the Middle East, and the deteriorated relationship that grew out of this racial hatred started by the Republican ideas on immigration and seclusion. The best way to summarize this was, keep Mexicans and Muslims out of the United States, and toss Christian beliefs on how to treat our brothers and sisters in Christ, out the window.

VII

Ever have that feeling of things just not being right? If i were a smarter man in the ways of situational awareness, I could have been much more in tuned with the things I was seeing, and put the puzzle pieces together much quicker. Afterall, who was I, just a college professor teaching History to people that were interested either in completing classes for graduation requirements or truly curious about the lynchpins in our civilization that triggered noteworthy periods and incidents in our society, good and bad. Never would I have thought that one little commencement speech been so pivotal. By teaching people how to think constructively, independently, critical and empathetic, I had unknowingly become a target of the Republican Party.

The assignment I gave, subsequent to my ass chewing, had intrigued some reporters that published a story on the inquiry as part of a more encompassing inquiry into the issue of Climate Change and how the Oil and Gas Industry has Legislators in their back pockets. Results showed a large swing in favor of voters electing Democrats and voting out Republicans in order to save our planet. They were tired of Republicans being deniers on the issue of Climate Change, even though the top scientist across the globe, NASA, and measurements taken from the International Space Station, all agree it was an issue of severe consequence. Only Republicans deny this issue because the Oil and Gas Industry give them money to ensure laws are made like the one made by the Oklahoma Legislature on the issue of Fracking.

Oklahoma was going to be a Blue State, meaning a Democratic State, and Republicans just could not have that.

It is probably a good thing I was unaware of being followed and monitored, because knowing my temperament and disposition I probably would have been much more confrontational and boisterous about the blatant hypocrisy that dwells on the right side of the aisle. But, silly me, I focused on challenging my students to think for themselves rather than believe what you see on television, especially FOX News. Hell, they were never right about anything! And how did they hate the mirror being put in front of their faces.

Time and time again the propaganda they were passing off as news was disproved by my students on a daily basis, it would seem that the few I had the pleasure of teaching fell more in line of being Independent rather than Democrat or Republican.

One philosophy I used to tell students was about those that had the "herd mentality". Land mammals that migrated in herds were always the prey, and the predators, though fewer in number, always capitalized on the herd by use of scare tactics and deception. Keeping the herd scared is how the predators always feed off their prey. And if you believed the bullshit on Fox News you stayed in a state of paranoia. Predators also eliminate any threat to the success of their kind.

In the African Plains, male lions will kill a hyena because they hunt the same prey. Hyenas greatly outnumber the lions, so when they show up en masse, the lions have no recourse but to retreat. And such was the ebb and flow of the existence of those class of predators. The herd was perpetually in a state of fear and unrest, and never developed the instinct of fight instead of flight. I challenged the herd to stampede the predators. Now I was challenging the right of the predator and making the existence of the prey one of peaceful dominance. (Time to evolve)

After one of these classroom "think tanks", as I liked to call them instead of class lectures, I saw this guy looking at me as I was walking to my car. It was eerie really because he was staring through the crowd, kinda as if he could see through the passer bys, faculty, students and employees, and see me. I opened my car door and jumped inside of my Prius and casually adjusted my mirrors. I slowly turned them to finally reveal where the strange man in the suit is, but he was gone. He had completely disappeared. I couldn't concentrate, there was this overwhelming feeling I was being watched. I pulled out of my parking space and began my usual drive home, it wasn't until fifteen minutes into the commute that I noticed a black SUV that kept making all the same lane changes as myself. I tried to slow down to see if I could get a closer look. I looked in my rear view mirror, and it was none other than the man that I saw when I was leaving the University. I knew I was being followed, and I began to panic. How am I supposed to get away? Do I accelerate and tip them off that I know they are following me? No, I could not do this, I still had too far to go to start racing through Durham. Think Plumb, think. I got it, right then I knew what to do. Up ahead there was an HOV crossover lane, I knew that if I could time it just right I could get into the HOV lane, then going down the highway losing those chasing me. Two miles to exit mark is when things became serious. I had to mentally prepare myself for what I was about to do, the turn was coming up. I predicted thirty seconds to when I would have to get over, I tried to wait as long as I could, the barricade/barrier was up ahead. Time was getting thin, ten seconds. Now, I had to go now. I turned the wheel sharply, screeching tires across traffic barely avoiding a car and the railway all together.

I glided into the lane, I regained control and looked back. The car tried to follow suit but unfortunately couldn't make the cross over and crashed into the barricade. Water went flying and a loud horn started blaring, I had escaped. But for how long I wonder. As soon as I could regain my thoughts and my senses, my mind went to one thing, Gabby.

I raced home to find my front door wide open. I swung the door open to find Gabby in the Kitchen talking to another man in a suit. I screamed, "what the hell are you doing in my home?" You don't have a warrant!" Automatic, in a drone like fashion, the man walked up to me and asked "are you professor Plumb?" "Yes, yes I am", I said. In his hands he had two pieces of paper, one a warrant the other a subpoena. In my mind I had to ask myself "Now why would the United States Government want to bring me in front of the court to testify, and about what? That's when it hit me, where did I teach? Duke University a publicly supported Koch funded institution. And what was I talking about in my "Think Tanks" was the Koch brothers and a new level of bought Government, just like in Oklahoma.

The dismantling of unions and less civil liberties, these are the basis of the REPUBLICAN AGENDA. Less, Government is what they preached. The truth is, they do not want less government, they want to control all of government! What I preached was the truth and so in turn I get persecuted for that. I say fuck that. Fuck them and fuck this subpoena, it was time to go and meet up with Jack.

Let me tell you about Jack. Jack Demirdjian was a lifelong friend of mine. We became friends during our Freshman year at San Diego State University. Because of his last name, he was looked at differently, like he single handedly orchestrated the takeover of the American Embassy himself. I was fortunate enough to have the last name Plumber, the fact that my mother was born in Iran was only known by a select group of people. I knew I would not think out of fear and spend my money in those industries that promoted fear like the NRA (Gun Nuts), and FOX News.

I had my mother's eye features, dark eyes, thick black eyebrows and long black eyelashes, but the name Plumber saved me from suspicion. Jack had no out. His name would be , the source of hatred based on the stereotypes Republicans gave Iranians. So naturally, being the humanitarian and open minded person that I am, I befriended him instantly. The tales of our stories are for another time, and what stories they are.

His field of study was Oceanography, and he was very adept at that study, very adept indeed. He would tell me of ocean currents, how they affected the Earth and mapping of the ocean floor. How important the oceans really are, and how Humans have deeply affected the planet. He was telling me that Scientists have even considered that we have created our own era for the planet, something that wasn't natural. They call it the "Anthropocene" age. The literal translation is "man-new", stemming from the from anthropo, for "man," and cene, for "new" because human-kind has altered the earth so drastically. Through mass extinctions of plant and animal species, mass pollution of the oceans and the atmosphere, we have created long lasting impacts for this planet.

We had a good exchange of knowledge. He was very curious as to the history of the United States also. How could a country so wealthy have so many sick, homeless and hungry people of its population. The more I explained how greed has corrupted our government and believe it is fine to lie to the American people. Initially, he thought I was a paranoid, conspiracy theory nut. But when I showed him proof of the allegations I was making, like using The Library of Congress, he began to think for himself and understand the truth in what I was learning.

Reaching Jack without compromising his anonymity was going to be a challenge. I had to rely on one night in a drunken stupor with this man, friend, brother from another mother, on this outlandish scenario how we would be there for each other in time of necessity.

We were out one night after our junior year, end of second semester at San Diego State University, during the "Cold War" era under President Reagan(R). Tensions were high on a global level as the United States, Russia and China all escalated the strength of their military might could muster. The threat of war was randomly tested by nations vying to protect and defend the territories of their countries, destroy and occupy if necessary to have peace through elimination and occupation. We got sick of listening to the constant fear being echoed by Republicans, and decided if things ever got too out of control, we would use the code phrase, "This is mutiny Mr. Christian". Jack always said it would be me who needed to use that since I was so outspoken about politics and one day I would piss the wrong person off. Even though I had the truth on my side, I found myself in the pickle that was Jack's' prediction.

While Gabby and I sat on the sofa, these agents were roaming through my house, and the guy standing over us was as stoic a figure as I have ever seen. He refused to answer any of my questions like, What is your name? What are you doing in my house? What am i being accused of? Why am i being followed? Why am i being investigated? Who do you work for? That was a question I was surprised to actually get a response to. When he said, "Homeland Security", I really got pissed! But just to let me know they had me by the short and curlies, he told me they would be gone before Laurie got home from the gym. I seriously had to clench my sphincter to stop myself from shitting my pants. How the hell could these guys come into my home and threaten the welfare of my family. Now my wife was being brought into this and I would not allow that to happen. First and foremost, I was my family's protector.

After they left I got a copy of the warrant and read it. These bastards were looking at me as if I were a Domestic Terrorist, and all I could surmise was that I openly spoke the truth about the racism and level of hatred that ran deep within the Republican Party. For example, Wake County in North Carolina, does that ring a bell to anyone?

My next class would be a whopper. If these guys did not like the information I was teaching, I would really give them a lesson they would love.

...Wake County was a County here in North Carolina, in the United States. The Koch brothers using their funds and connections put two School Board Administrators in office. No one pays attention to the minor elections, but the Koch Brothers do. Using their money and influence, the Koch Brothers were then able to enact a bill that then in turn made segregation legal again. How? They funded the campaigns of two candidates, then once elected, they used their influence to create laws that would stop busing. This caused an uproar among the community. People came together in force to battle this level of tyranny. The playbook that these brothers used, once segregation was deemed unconstitutional they coined terms like "forced busing" and "neighborhood schools". They used these terms to make segregation legal without having to break the law. These brothers had no knowledge of morales and human decency. All they see and know is the bottom line, that bottom line, money. Another perfect example of how the Republicans that ran my state of North Carolina. **All for getting on their knees and wrapping their lips around Koch brother money.**

"Profesor, where do you learn this information?", came from a male student. I did not even have to reply, a female student in the class retorted, "Just google Wake County School Board Elections, it is all there!"

...here is a little history on the Koch brothers. These guys made their money primarily in the oil and gas industries. Which means, they had the supply the world needed, and made billions of dollars in profit by the fiscal quarter. They funded Republicans in Congress and the Senate to secure laws that would benefit not only them but the wealthiest people in the United States. For example, every time you went to the gas pump to fill your car with gasoline, part of the taxes on the gas paid at the pump went to them for upkeep on pipelines and other hardware necessary to facilitate sucking the resources from the earth. And of course they paid no tax on the revenue collected from the taxes collected from consumers at the pump. What they did with these gross piles of revenue is what makes these bastards despicable. Not only were they responsible for the story in Wake County as described above, they tried to buy every federal, state, and local political offices to promote their agenda.

...these guys were behind the economic philosophy of the Reagan administration, or "Reaganomics". Reaganomics was simple, give the tax breaks to the rich and make the middle and low class people pay the line share for the rich. The money flowed freely from the hands of the Koch brothers and the like, to politicians lining up to screw over working Americans for "dirty money". They rigged and bought the political system so only the wealthy had opportunities. These miscreants created the nonsensical idea of minimal skilled jobs to justify suppressing their employees wages. There was never any legislation passed regarding that issue, it was just another ploy to stick it to the American worker, ie, make the slave work harder so the plantation master makes more money. Now that we know how our country lost being a Democracy and became an Oligarchy, the discussion on how far Republicans went to create a division between the rich and poor in the United States, foreign policy issues that surround greed and how unilaterally they thought they could do what no one else in the history of man had ever accomplished, they wanted to take over the world. Capitalism would be the plantation, and every employee across the globe would work the plantation.

I decided to end class early that day, there was so much on my mind I really felt like all the information I wanted to impart had been given. There were more important things for me to think about now.
I had to escape the plantation, but how? Think Plumb, think. I knew that because of the Patriot Act there would be no way I could make a move without being noticed. It was obvious I was being followed and monitored, along with my family. How else would Homeland Security know to send an agent that was proficient in sign language? How would they know where my wife was, and myself for that matter and come to our home when just Gabby was there. She was a smart girl, but even she knew not to make things difficult if the feds showed up at your door. Getting myself and my family off the grid would be an exceptional challenge. I thought, how am i going to leave everything behind and sustain a life for the ones i promised to always provide for? This would be a trick even Houdini would marvel at.

My plan would have to required loyalty, timing, stealth and more luck than the Irish had in reserves. Navigating my way out with no expectation of privacy anymore, I had to act a if there was no sense of urgency in my mannerisms, maintain my composure around friends, family and colleagues. Most importantly, how was I going to contact Jack without having him monitored as well. It would do none of us any good to both be tracked and wanted by the feds. Then it hit me, I would go public, go on the offensive and put Congress and Republicans on their heels instead of cowering like a little girl. I might be on my way to the Bataan Death March, but I would do my best to land a good punch before being led to slaughter.

I knew my first move. I had to have a press conference, a conference that would not only reach the public but inform it. As soon as the agent had left the house, I ran down   the stairs and went to my office. I went inside and went immediately to my desk table. I remembered a student that I once had that is now an affiliate investigative reporter of MSNBC , let's say she was one of my favorite students. This woman never backed down from an issue, she always stood her ground, she fought for what was right. She engaged in such activities as objectively covering the Republican threat of another government shutdown over the issue of Planned Parenthood.

Planned Parenthood was under attack by Republicans in Congress to show the depths of their conservatism. The big lie perpetrated by Republican lawmakers and broadcast all over FOX News was that Planned Parenthood was using taxpayer money for abortions, and abortions were just a total abomination as far as they were concerned. They Tried to make women feel less than human by exercising their constitutional rights to abort a pregnancy if the woman felt it was in her best interest to do so. Abortion was the law of the land, but remember, those on the right felt the law did not apply, as long it differed from the opinions they held, what anyone else wanted was immaterial. Anyway, I could go on about how big this hypocrisy went. Let us not forget, Republicans were the party of "less government", yet they wanted to use government to affect and restrict the rights of over half the population of the United States, women.

I closed the door to my office, picked up the phone and started to dial. Erica picked up the phone after a few rings, I am still surprised I still remember the number. There was some silence and then I heard her voice "Hello?". Hello is this Erica Velasquez? "Yes, who's this?", She replied. "Hi Erica, this is Professor Plumb." "How can I help you", she asked. "Well Erica, I kind of have a problem. I need to get in front of a camera and on National News. Can you make that happen? "Yes" she said, "do you mind me asking why?" "Let's just say it involves an infringement of rights of the First Amendment." She asked me what i meant by that and I had to think fast. Eventually this would go public and be on all the major news covering media outlets, television, radio, newspaper, social media and last but not least, gossip. I had to be in control of how this made others think of their right to Free Speech, so I swung for the fences. "I found federal agents in my home today while only my deaf daughter was home, Reader's Digest version, I have been subpoenaed to appear before the congressional oversight committee on terrorism, by Homeland Security agents. I have to appear before Congress this coming February.

That really struck a chord with her because she wanted an exclusive interview before any other media had a chance to grill me with possible questions I might be posed with from Congress. Think faster Plumb! I knew that if I ever needed an ally that the media would be ace in the hole, how low did I have to go survive. Now the one outlet I really was in judgement of was how the media put a spin on things just for ratings and not so much for the pure truth that lies at the heart of an issue. What other choice really did I have? Well, I called her, right? Here it goes Plumb, I thought, let me get my side out first through the media, another First Amendment protected class, we had that in common so I ran with it. "Erica, I'll give you the exclusive, but you have to promise me something." "What is that?" she asked. " I would like for you to be at the conference and ask the first question targeting this issue." If I did not control how the media spun this I could really be in trouble. FOX News would spin this as if I were a Domestic Terrorist because I was against the social views of the far right wing thinkers of the Republican Party. "What question might that be professor?" "Not over the phone, come to my house and we will speak privately. You may bring a recording device if you like, but come alone please." She had one stipulation of her own, "I get to ask the follow up question to the one you want asked first." Smart girl, she took our think tanks to heart.

Ooh, good job Plumb, way to be mysterious. If I did not try to find some humor in this, at least in the privacy of my own head, I am sure I would give myself an ulcer. We agreed and settled on a good time that would suit both of our schedules. We had to act fast, time was of the essence. Fifteen minutes, 15 minutes -- all the time in the world right? Yeah, I believe so. Like any nerve racking situation I've ever encountered during my lifetime my bowels started becoming active. Now that this was done I asked myself, what would be the first question I want asked at the press conference? It was painfully obvious, from this moment on I would have to rely on quick decisions and spontaneity. One of two things was evident, Erica would catapult her career and I would be able to relocate my family, or we would all die a mysterious death...thrilling. I laughed when I thought of "sleeping with the fishes" as my fate, little did I know how true that would play out.

The first question would have to be an attention getter, but not too revealing. I figured a good opener would be a simple "why you?". I would have to answer this question with such clarity that my message would put the Republican led Congress on their heels. Calling a spade a spade would be my tactic. Since Republicans got control of Congress in 2000, they have used that branch of government to bully and browbeat anyone that had a different opinion on social issues like, Minimum Wage, Planned Parenthood, Social Security, Healthcare, Taxes, Assistance for the Underprivileged, Gun Safety Legislation, Immigration, National Defense Spending, and probably the most pressing issue, Climate Change.

Naturally this was just political partisanship, Republican Congressional members would talk or shout over the citizens they subpoenaed, interrupt testimony and not let the person sworn to testify to the truth get a word in edgewise. I think we all remember the Planned Parenthood meeting where several Republican Congressmen were grilling the President of planned Parenthood, Cecile Richards.

If they didn't like the answers starting to be given, then they would simply turn the microphone off and talk over them, sometimes yell, to silence any point of view they did not agree with. I could go on and on, but let us just give this analogy, Republicans acted like sore losers when things did not go their way, they acted like kids in the schoolyard that wanted to take their ball home because they lost or were losing.

After John Boehner(R), Speaker of the House, resigned his position and seat in Congress, the most inexperienced member of Congress was elected to the speaker's position. Kevin McCarthy(R), on his first day announcing his bid for the Speaker of the House job, gave a press conference admitting to these oversight committees were nothing more that a political ploy to hurt Democrats in future elections. He Called out Democratic candidate Hillary Clinton by name, saying she was the target because she was the favorite of the political pundits to get the nomination on the Democratic ticket. For over two years Republicans hung their hat on the issue of Benghazi. Thank God he did not wind up with the Speakership, that honor went to Rep. Paul Ryan(R), from Wisconsin.

Four Americans died in a terroristic attack on the Embassy compound in Benghazi, a terrible tragedy. Over two years, Republicans badmouthed and accused President Obama and Secretary of State, Hillary Clinton, of being negligent where Benghazi was concerned. They were bashed on FOX News and every conservative mouthpiece they could find, even fat ass Rush Limbaugh. My question is, when were Republicans ever going to investigate the 13 Americans that died in Foreign Embassies in 54 attacks during the Bush Administration. The answer, never, because Republicans were not concerned about possible wrongdoings within their own party. I am just waiting for the pictures of Senate Arms Committee Chair, John McCain(R), and the head of ISIS, the ultimate terroristic organization on the planet, to arise. Oh wait, they already have. McCain in 2013 was in the news saying, "We need to arm and train ISIS because they are the key to beating the Assad regime in Syria, because Assad poses the greatest threat to our national security." In 2014, McCain was again in the news ranting, "We need to arm and train the Syrian rebels to fight ISIS because they pose the greatest threat to our national security." Now they were trying to lump me in with that organization because they were losing their grip on government.

This might answer the question of how ISIS is getting the weapons they need. If little old me can see this and wonder why this is happening, certainly Congress with the resources they have can see it. Run away Boehner! There are things that truly need investigating, and you wasted my taxpayer dollars on this partisanship. All this time I thought the Constitution said the job of Congress was to represent the people that elected them to office, but Republicans used it as a weapon against Democrats or anyone else that thought Christianity applied to everyone else but themselves. Yes, this would be how I would open the press conference.

When the doorbell rang I thought all the blood ran from my body and I would drop to the floor, Had fifteen minutes gone by that fast? No, only six minutes had past, who was at my door. When I gazed through the peephole in the door I saw it was Erica. I opened the door and she went by me so fast i felt like i was in a draft. "First rule of journalism professor, never give your interviewee a chance to back out, I do apologize for being so early".

She did come alone as I asked, that was a relief. I did not worry about her being bugged since I consented to be recorded, so I exhaled and welcomed her into our home.

Being the gracious host that I am, i offered her a drink but she was eager to get to work. I sensed this story was going to be a big deal to her so I took a hunch that she would hang on my every word, she was a good person. I told her everything, and I was astonished to hear her response. She confided in me that there have been some protesters outside their office building because they spoke out against the Confederate Flag. The thing that struck a nerve with these ignorant sons of bitches wanting to display that piece of shit banner because the big boss of the station compared the citizens of Germany to those of the Confederate States, or the Bible Belt states of this era. She said "at least the people of Germany recognize what their flag under Hitler represented, and banned that flag in perpetuity, due to the millions of Jews that were murdered under that flag, but the people in the southern states continue to cling to the symbol that said "slavery was the biggest economic source of revenue" and that is what that flag of the Confederate States and that flag represented". How true is that! I thought, they could not wait to display their love of racism. Hypocrites,all of them in my opinion.

"Well, you are right" I told her, "I have seen my share of it here in North Carolina just about as much as anywhere else in the "red" Bible Belt states. But I am sure you did not come here to talk about protestors in front of your building". "I am not so sure", she said, "ever since the Supreme Court gutted the Civil Rights Bill of 1965, we have been getting copious amounts of people complaining to us about being denied the right to vote. Our station has been broadcasting these stories to show the people of America that racism was not dead simply because we had a Black President. As a matter of fact, it became more evident by the way President Obama was treated by FOX News. They aired such propaganda as: is he a citizen? where is his birth certificate? can we trust the one he finally provided? Better yet was it authentic? This was gold. These tactics were racist, pure and simple. Never in the history of the United States of America was a President prior to President Obama asked to show proof of their citizenship. Why? Because all of them were White".

Donald Trump began this absurd rhetoric, I thought, and this was the frontrunner for most of the primary season during the presidential campaign in the Republican Party. But every other candidate has spoken about their doubts as well, all for some of that Koch Brother money we talked about earlier. It is a recurring theme.

Erica was a chatter box, talking about how this voter issue has been affecting North Carolina and how it all stems from Governor McCrory's legislation enacting old laws that made it hard if not impossible for Black people to vote. There is no doubt this was a racist move on the Governor's part, since an overwhelming majority of Black voters cast their ballot for Democrats. Proof positive that restricting the Constitutional right of voting to people not White was very much alive. In my opinion, and also the majority of Americans, Clarence Thomas, the only African-American on the Supreme Court was the ultimate, how do I put this kindly... "house nigger" if you will. It would appear Clarence forgot that not long ago, his marriage to a White woman was illegal in the United States. A more progressive thinking court ruled that marriages of people of different ethnic backgrounds was deemed legal, but he had his eyes set all over Republican money and made legal decisions not in the best interest of Americans, but for big business and big money. He was definitely a "house nigger"!!!! through and through. What a sell out.

I reminded her on our think tank regarding the issue of power, and how those that use corruption to obtain power will use that power corruptly. She said it was one of her favorite class discussions, and how it led her to the world of Journalism, to be the voice of the truth, and report it not on the basis of political agenda, but simply for the truth. I was very proud of her.

I could not believe it, by her talking about what was going on in her world of history as it happens, she made me feel much calmer, now I was ready to tell her my story and pray she did not think I was going to be an ant shy of a picnic.

After I told her about finding the feds in my living room and the subpoena, I noticed she had stopped writing and was staring at me, mouth agape. Of course the part about sending the coded message to Jack was omitted, the less she knew the better, and she told me she would do her best to get the media and a camera in front of me.

VIII

When Laurie got home, she was her usual giddy and happy self, I knew breaking this news to her would terrify her. Nothing brought out the ferocity in that woman until someone messed with Gabby. She was not a helicopter parent, but she stayed aware of her daughter's whereabouts and who she was with while giving her the space to grow and develop her social skills. She also was great with Gabby because she was very nurturing with ther but also allowed her to make her own mistakes, all the while knowing the right time to intervene before any catastrophe had an opportunity to make an entrance. I loved watching that woman parent, she was the best.

After we talked, drank whatever wine was in the house to calm our nerves, we had an outline of a plan. During the next few months, we would downsize as much as possible with material possessions, stockpile the back of the minivan with enough water and toilet paper as possible without drawing undue attention to ourselves. Deodorant, toothpaste, dental floss, other toiletries were small enough to fit in a backpack or big purse or any shoulder strap bag for at least a six month time period. Snacks like crackers, nuts, hard candy, chips, cookies, trail mix, gum, mints and things like that were small enough to store in the mini as well. We could do this a little at a time and keep the attention to a minimum. If we were going to be watched, I did not want to send any alerts or out of character mannerisms that would put my family in danger.

What surprised me was how fast I heard back from Erica. Her boss was so eager to broadcast the press conference the next morning. "News does not wait" she said, "Tiffany is anxious to punch some Republicans in the mouth and she is happy to give you your fifteen minutes of fame". Tiffany Clements, the head of the station, was a straight shooter Erica told me, she walks the walk. If anyone stood on the side of equity it was her, and it was obvious by the unbiased coverage of current events and direct and plain English interviews her staff conducted. It truly did not matter, Republican or Democrat, everyone was treated with respect and still were asked the hardline questions that needed to be asked and covered.

In all the hoopla, I never asked Erica what her follow-up question was going to be. I would just answer truthfully, there was no other choice really. It seemed she was on my side, so I decided not to worry on my mistake and focus on the speech I would make in the morning.

IX

*Good morning ladies, gentlemen, members of the press
and those of you watching now or listening later. I hope
to keep this as brief as possible, but being a Teacher
please keep in mind I do talk for a living (smile Plumb)*

*What I have to say is very important because it is my
opinion that our First Amendment rights are being
challenged by those seeking to impose their beliefs on us
without any regard for anyone that speaks openly in
opposition to them. When I say them, I mean
Republicans in Congress and the Senate, which are the
majority party, and still use subterfuge to maintain that
power. Subterfuge like voter suppression, mass
incarceration of Americans for non violent offenses, or
basically victimless crimes like marijuana possession. If
you ask me, anyone that was arrested for cocaine should
be given a full pardon and the right to vote restored to
them.*

*Cocaine is grown in Central America and the Southern
Hemisphere,not in the United States. Furthermore, you
can not grow cocaine. You have to grow the cocoa leaf
and process the leaf to get cocaine from it. But I digress,
the definition of entrapment is to get someone to commit
a crime that they are not predisposed to commit.
Therefore if cocaine is not a product of North America, is
had to be shipped here in mass quantities via, boat,
plane, train or other methods of huge distribution. The
facts have already been exposed that it was the CIA who
brought this dug into the country in the quantities*

sufficient to distribute it nationwide in every major city, town and hub of trafficking in the United States. Since cocaine was a felony to possess, anyone convicted of possession has had their voice removed from society. Surprisingly enough, it is the African-American communities that populate the prison system for this crime, can you say voter suppression? I thought that you could.

(that got a rumble from the crowd)

I submit to you that silencing people from their right to vote is taking their free speech from them, and these laws in place, such as here in North Carolina enacted by Governor McCrory, violate the First Amendment of our Constitution on free speech, notwithstanding the Fifteenth Guaranteeing every citizen the right to vote.

I have made my living educating those thirsting for the truth on how to recognize the truth when it makes its presence known. Because of that, I came home yesterday to find Federal Agents in my house with my deaf daughter, a 13 year old, executing a search warrant and subpoenaing me to testify before Congress on the issue of Domestic Terrorism.

The lengths our Government is going to - to try and silence the people is astounding. 1984, Animal Farm, Idiocracy... All of these great pieces have a single common occurrence, Government Oppression. This is exactly what is happening to me right now, as we speak. As I stand here I can't help but think is my family safe, my friends... Am I safe? Time and time again we have seen the lengths that these tyrants will go to, to silence and eliminate those that disagree with them. Even as I say these things I fear for my own well being. Will I be a headline of tomorrow's paper? Or just another blip of history, forgotten and not remembered.

For instance, they accomplished this silence by gutting the Voting Rights Act of the Civil Rights Act of 1965. How? According the the Voting Rights section of the law, any changes in law regarding voting had to be submitted to the Attorney General of the United States. By gutting that portion of the law, states no longer had to meet that requirement. Within a day of that decision, the states across the Bible belt began enacting voter ID laws and making the act of registering to vote impossible for millions of Americans. So someone like my father, who was born in the United States, voted his entire life, worked his entire life, but now cannot drive due to glaucoma taking his vision, does not have a driver's license now cannot vote? According to Republicans, yes. Why would they want to do this? Because he gets Social Security, he paid into it his entire life, but Republicans want to cut the program. Naturally, my father would vote Democrat to make sure that does not happen. Voter suppression is the only thing voter ID laws intend to accomplish.

Denying a citizen of this country the right to register to vote is blatantly racist since White people have never been denied the right to register to vote. In Texas, birth certificates are being denied to children that are born in this country because either one or both of the parents was born in Mexico, not just another country, specifically Mexico. That is just Racism 101. **(Beginning racism for those of you that are unfamiliar with college jargon)**

In Alabama, the voter ID law changed to require citizens to have a state issued identification card. Yet in the last presidential election, only ten of the counties in that state voted majorily for President Obama. Alabama closed eight county offices that issue driver's licenses and identification cards in ten of those counties. Not one office was closed in any county that voted for Mitt Romney. It is painfully obvious the Supreme Court got this ruling wrong. **(All with the help of that ultimate house nigger Clarence Thomas. He should have been cast in the roll of Stephen instead of Samuel Jackson in the movie "Django")**

And yet the powers that be, the Republican led Congress, knowingly stand by do absolutely nothing because the Constitution they were sworn to uphold meant absolutely nothing to them. Not one member of Congress has brought forth legislation protecting the rights of those infringed upon because of the lame excuse that "the votes are not there".

According to 1 Timothy 6:10, the love of money is the root of all evil, and the hub of that root is Washington D.C. WE live in an Oligarchical society, where the wealthy control power by owning our legislators, and I am not naive enough to not believe our Supreme Court is also on the payroll after the "Citizens United" decision. **(Yes, the Supreme Court house nigger was part of that ruling in favor of big money)**

As far as I am concerned, the love of money is tantamount to nothing but greed, and greed is one of the seven deadly sins.

Luke 6:24-26, "Woe unto you that are rich! Woe unto you that are full! for you shall hunger. Woe unto you that laugh now, for you shall weep. Woe unto you, when all men shall speak well of you! for so did their fathers to the false prophets."

If Americans would realize that what we have now is "taxation without representation" then collectively we could have a peaceful revolution. Vote! What is choking our Democracy is "Apathy"! The lack of desire to believe change for the betterment of our society is achievable. But nothing is farther from the truth. The belief is that the President is the most powerful person in the country, nope. But that is when the largest turnout for elections occur, and that turnout is pitiful. The truth of the matter is that local elections are far more important, as shown in the school board elections of Wake County here in North Carolina a few years ago.

The important elections are Secretary of State because that is who is responsible for elections in your states. State legislators, because that is who dicates laws in your states, not the President. Congress and Senate, because that is who has the responsibility for enacting federal laws, not the President. The only authority the President has as far as laws in this country are the ones presented to him by Congress. And if the President initiates legislation, it is Congress and the Senate that have to agree and vote on it before the President can sign off on it and make it law. Wake up people!

They are holding us hostage by shutting the government down and infringing on our rights, making us submit our rights in order to refund the government for their agenda. You cant disagree with the owner of the red ball on the playground because he will go home. Which is why I would not be surprised when the Government announced a shutdown due to the inability to defund Planned Parenthood. Just like when they shutdown the Government in the past due to Obamacare. But do you really think Planned Parenthood is the real issue when the Iran Nuclear deal was also occurring. The Iran deal has worldwide implications. But before we talk about this current dilemma, take a walk down memory lane with me.

How did Iran acquire its nuclear technology? In 1953, under the leadership of President Dwight Eisenhower, the United States gave it to them!

That is correct, the first nuclear centrifuge in Iran was built by the United States.

Now, with the state of affairs in the Middle East as tense as they are, Republicans unanimously oppose the brokered deal with the United States, Iran, Russia, China, France, Germany and Great Britain. The entire United Nations unanimously ratified this historical agreement because they understand what the implications could be if this agreement collapsed.

The entire nuclear technological community even agree that this is not a perfect deal, no deal ever is, but if this agreement were adhered to then Iran would be prevented from obtaining nuclear weapons.

But you cannot tell a Republican politician anything because they were in this for one reason, sabotage anything President Obama supported, those guys are very childish and vindictive. Look at how they treated the head of Planned Parenthood, Cecile Richards. For almost five hours, they tried to get her to admit to wrongdoing in that organization. Chairman of the oversight committee, and also candidate for Speaker of the house, Jason Chaffetz(R), led the charge on Ms. Richards asking questions about how Planned Parenthood profits from abortions (which is a lie), to her salary. Never in the history of Congress has a man been asked his salary, but this was blatant evidence of the war Republicans waged on women.

I apologize for rambling, but I know when I get in front of Congress they will pull this playbook out on me and I will be treated like a lamb led out to slaughter. Please indulge me a few more minutes of your time.

In the nearly two years that these negotiations have been going, Iran has fulfilled their responsibility of the agreement to not enrich uranium to weapon like capacity, and with the world watching and the nations that hammered out this deal, it would be unlikely Iran will violate the terms and conditions of this nuclear deal.

I have to say that I strongly believe if Republicans cause the United States to renege on this agreement then the nuclear fallout that is likely to occur will destroy mankind on a global level.

This is mutiny Mr. Christian!

Erica jumped to her feet and shouted, "Why you Professor?" I could not make myself out to be pompous, so I calmly answered, "The only reason I can give you is because they want to silence me and discredit my name. that is the Republican playbook. And that is the reason i support Sen. Bernie Sanders(I), from Vermont." She did not miss a beat with her follow up question, no reporter in the room stood a chance to get a word in over her. Why do you support someone that believes in Socialism?" In the Bible Belt states, any mention of Socialism is compared with Communism, which are two totally different things. My reply came off without any hint of fear in speaking in favor of what Socialism really is. "Most of the things Americans love most were born from socialist movements in the country. All of us in this room have loved ones that rely on government programs such as Social Security, the only government run health insurance plan for Senior Citizens and people with Disabilities. Minimum Wage was born from a social movement to provide working Americans with a wage sufficient to live on without having to rely on government assistance." The room fell hush, it was my opportunity to continue to educate.

The days off Working Americans enjoy, those Saturdays and Sundays, were the result of Union support and negotiations. Yet in Wisconsin, Governor Scott Walker(R), takes pride in destroying the champion of the worker, the ones that make America run. whatever Unions have turned into today, their function at conception was solely to ensure the rights of the workers were represented. Does there need to be reform, yes, there are people who abuse the system, but they are in the vast minority. The great majority of workers that go to work everyday rely on the protection of their jobs to keep a roof over the head of their families and putting food on the table. Taking away their protections are tantamount to opening the door to the chicken coup for the foxes to run in at will (that is at will employment) And the horse you rode in on Governor!

Medicare, It is called an entitlement because you are entitled after having paid into it your whole working life! All of our parents, uncles, aunts, brothers, sisters, cousins, close friends and neighbors that have families and so on, rely on this for their healthcare and well being. Medicare was also born from a Socialist movement in this country. None of us want to see it go away or be cut for that reason, yet every Republican wants to cut it. The only reason they cannot cut it now is because President Obama would veto any legislation that aims to cut benefits for these people, and the disabled, that rely on its existence. Yet all Republicans claim to be running on a moral platform, they are all hypocrites as far as I am concerned. The truth is, if we had a single *payer system for healthcare in this country, the fiscal deficit would drop severely because the responsibility of unpaid medical bills would no longer fall on the taxpayers of this country. And for those of you that want to diminish the health care the citizens of Canada receive as a result of this program, it may have started on a rocky path, just like medicare, medicare part D, Romneycare in Massachusetts and the Affordable Healthcare Act. After thirty years of being in service, the citizens of Canada are very pleased with the quality of healthcare they receive, and doctors make on average of over $300,000 annually. No one is complaining. As a matter of fact, they look at us like we are stupid for having health care based on an insurance system rather than single payer. maybe taxes are a little high in Canada to pay for this, but the population is only thirty million.*

In the United States the population is over 300 million, there is a much larger tax base to draw from in this country, so the cost per citizen, per capita, would be far less than what a Canadian citizen pays.

Social Security, another Social program that millions of retired Americans rely on for income during the period in life when Father Time says you have worked enough. The lie broadcast on FOX News on a daily basis by Republicans is that Social Security is going bankrupt. The facts totally dispute the propaganda on that issue however. In actuality, there is a two trillion dollar surplus in that program. Republicans just want to get their hands on it and take away the security millions have each month and want retirees to invest instead in the volatility of the American and Global Markets.

Which do you prefer for your loved ones?

So if investing in the safety and security of the citizens of the United States is considered Socialism, then I am on board.

Erica sat down, grin on her face and I could tell grateful for acquiring national exposure. Her question was brilliant, she asked in such a way that would gain the support of the idiot rednecks, but allow the response in such a way that a civilized answer could be be given. Hands went up all over the room, questions were being yelled around the room in such a manner that all that could be heard was the inaudible sounds of reporters. Lights were flashing at a rapid pace from angles across the room. It was hard to see anything with any distinction because of the brightness of the flashes and the sea of hands waving throughout the room, hiding all those but that were in the front row. I looked as bet I could for the most hateful face in the crowd I could make out. Bingo! There he was, a red faced, senior citizen, veins bulging from the sides of his neck, sweat encircling the collar of his white business, button down shirt, gut sticking out from between his sport coat because he did not dare try and button it for fear of one of those buttons launching from his jacket like an RPG from the force of his belly that would not be contained. The buttons on his shirt were already screaming as it is.

"What makes you think you can come down here and tarnish our heritage by labeling North Carolina and the God fearing Conservative people across the south as people who are against common decency?!

In my Christian view, I choose to believe in the words of Jesus Christ, who gave us the model in which to govern our lives by. John 15:12, "This is my commandment, That you love one another, as I have loved you."

How did Jesus love us? He healed the sick, he fed the poor, he taught us how to treat our fellow man through parables, and the only thing he asked of us was to love Him and no other God, and to love one another. Judge not, lest you be judged, live by the sword die by the sword, turn the other cheek, whatever you do for the least of my brethren you have done for Me. Those were the principals I was taught to live by. And if you pay attention, it is a Commandment! A directive on how we should treat our fellow man. Anything that is in opposition with that Commandment I refuse to support.

The noise level in the room rose to a point that I felt really in touch with just how much hatred was permeating throughout the south. It was clear to me this press conference was over, no one was interested in hearing a positive message, they were too engulfed in perpetuating the racist heritage they were taught by their ancestors. Members of the press were trying to gather around me, shoving microphones in my face, shouting questions that could not be heard over the crowd that was unwilling to open their minds and hear the hard realities of current and past events. To them, anything not White was wrong.

I swung my head, searching for an exit sign, it was time to make an contrails out of this place. Having someone try to take a cheap shot at you is not my idea of a good time, and it was apparent with mobs like these, that was not out of the realm of possibility. After all, in the southern states (Bible Belt) people were known to come up missing from being lynched, drowned in a swamp and left for alligator bait, beaten within an inch of your life. Just because the Civil Rights Act was passed, a majority of people in this country were under the impression racism was over with, haha, wrong! I was not taking any chances.

It was then i nearly lost it. "There, I shouted!" I pointed across the room where I had just spotted the agent that was in my home serving the warrant with Just Gabby home. "There is the agent that was in my home!" Only the closest reporters to me could hear my alert, they turned to see, but none of them knew who to look for. If he was leaving since i spotted him, he knew the way out, and I was going to follow him. One, to get the hell out of here, and two, to find out why he was following me, and who else was in on it?

Due to true southern hospitality form, I had cups of coffee thrown at me, along with other mysterious liquids, paper, food, and anything else a mob could hurl. Maneuvering through the aisles trying to get out of this mayhem was challenging to say the least. I almost tripped on a chair that was pushed in front of me. I thought about picking it up and wielding it like a hammer to create space, but the only thing the mob would give me was a shield against any crazed redneck that might take the opportunity to shoot. These nut jobs loved guns. Thank God a few reporters stuck by me while trying to get out as well, they kept the first volley that were being thrown just out of reach to prevent any serious blows from meeting their mark, I was not in the mood for a concussion. After all,I am an old man, fifty five years of age, arthritic and a total pacifist at heart, unless it came to my family. Even though I stand over six feet in height and weigh 200+ pounds, in no way do I ever try to display a confrontational manner, unless absolutely necessary .

Today however was one of those days where you had to dig deep to summon a little bravado for yourself. I tried to keep in some sort of shape, solely for the purpose of not keeping my heart in optimal functioning conditions. The closer to the door we inched, that bravado came at a great time. I bent my knees, leaned forward and pushed everyone out of the way that my armspan and strength could allow. It was good enough to push the door open, and just when I thought I had gotten out of there pretty fortunately under the circumstances, a bottle crashed squarely into the back of my skull. I felt just like Daffy Duck seeing a bright light quickly encompass my vision completely for a half a second. At least I was still on my feet, exit stage left!

I came too and shut the door, trapping all of those behind me. Thank you again to the Reporters and Citizens that helped me escape, I thought I was off scot free but guess again. Who was standing outside the door waiting for me none other than Mr. Agent himself. Not at all what I was expecting when I regained control of my sight, quickly he punched me in the solar plexus knocking the wind out of me. When I started to come to, the other hand caught me right on the jaw with an uppercut, and this time it was lights out. When I came to my senses, I realized I was in the back seat of a sedan with Mr. Agent sitting next to me. We were in front of my house and the driver had opened the door so I could get out. I asked Mr. Agent what that was for and he told me, "you are a professor, supposed to be a smart guy, figure it out. Now get out". When I asked him if I could at least have his name he said, "I am sure you have seen a spy movie or two in your life professor, pick any name you like and I will answer to it".

Now I am an educated man, you would think I can learn a lesson since I craft them for a living. But under the circumstances I felt the asshole in me racing way ahead of better judgement and said, "Dickhead it is". The driver must have had a blackjack or something because all I felt was a tug on my jacket collar, then a revisiting to the spot on my head where the bottle had found its mark. Once again I found myself waking up not in my bed, but on my front lawn, head pounding and Laurie and Gabby standing over me. All Laurie said was, "let's go, I am taking you to the emergency room". Sweeter words were never spoken.

On the way to the hospital, Laurie was making sure I was alright. she kept water in her car,and it was probably the only thing she had to offer hoping dehydration would not make a concussion any worse. I played along of course, she was trying hard to hold it together so I did not try my usual attempts at humor to ease her concern. I also did not want to freak her out even more by telling her that her car might be bugged, so I waited for the right opportunity to tell her how I really felt about what we should do.

When we arrived at the emergency room, it felt like a civilian M.A.S.H. unit. There were children with coughs, snot running down their noses, an elderly person on an oxygen tank, a teenager with what appeared to be a broken arm, a man with a laceration on his forehead, pressing a t-shirt to it trying to stop the bleeding, and the list went on. We saw the triage nurse and got checked in, and I figured this was as good and safe a time to tell Laurie and Gabby what I felt we needed to do next. Surely the emergency waiting room was not bugged.

X

We were on the same page now, it was time to get out of Dodge. These guys knew how to send a message, and it was coming through, crystal clear. Anything I had to say was not important if it meant the safety of myself and my family.

It took four hours of waiting before I finally was taken into a room to be examined. Three head x-rays and five stitches later, I was finally discharged. At least there was no skull fracture, mom always said I had a hard head, lol. Laurie drove home, parked the car in the garage, turned on the alarm system and put me to bed. The drugs they gave me for pain at the hospital were awesome. Within minutes I was unconscious, allowing all the aches in my body to heal as much as possible and hope the pain will have dissipated by morning, late morning!

I remember thinking as I was drifting off, *I really must be on the money with this and they will do anything to keep people from exposing them.*

Sleep did not get the time it needed to be of much help in aiding with my pain relief. Standing over me, about 2a.m. was a man holding a gun with a silencer on it, pointing it at my forehead. He held his index finger to his puckered lips signifying for me to be quiet. How do you argue with a man who makes such a persuasive gesture? After the events of the previous day I decided to shut the wise ass up inside of me and just follow directions. He removed his finger from his lips and motioned for me to get out of bed and follow him. Good thing I sleep in a t-shirt and my underwear, this could not get any worse, could it? I felt, here is the hammer stroke, the alarm did not stop this person from intruding my home at this hour of the day and the ultimatum of "shut up or you and your family are going to have an accident speech" was around the corner.

The mystery man motioned for me to go downstairs, naturally I cooperated,at least to this point there was no plastic tarp lining the floor in my house anywhere. He motioned for me to get into the bathroom leading out to the garage, and he stepped in with me. "I am sorry" he said, "I cannot take the risk of exposing myself before this. Your house is bugged, and this is the only safe room in the house to whisper in."

"You can call me John, it is a name you can say without anyone reading your lips." He went on to tell me that I had really made some people mad with the information that I have been disseminating lately, and that everything I had been saying was true. There are very powerful people that want you out of the way. Yesterday was just a warning, a serious one, and even your lecture hall at Duke is bugged. They will not hesitate to kill you and your family.

Who would go to such lengths to want me dead? I am just a teacher, I told him. "That stunt of a press conference you pulled yesterday is all over the news, reporters are licking their chops for an exclusive after everything that happened and the powers that be want your lips shut, permanently." "Jack sent me to get all of you out of here, but it will not be as easy as just walking away from here." Whoever John is, he is a professional. He explained that I could not disappear when I have a summons to appear before Congress. I was being watched, and more than likely the media would be camped outside my house for a while. "You guys have enough food in the house to last at least two weeks, lay low and wait to hear from me."

Finally, he told me to turn our cell phones and computers off, do not answer the house phone and he would be in touch. I told him I had to pee, and he winked at me, I will be right back, do not look for me after you have washed your hands. By this point I turned into a robot, following instructions instead of being my own man anymore. Slowly I ascended the stairs to return to bed, my head thumping with every step. By the time I climbed back in bed, all I could think about was, "How did Jack get the message while in the middle of the ocean, and how did he know to send a frigging ninja?" Did I really know Jack? At this point he was definitely better than the alternative. Plus, he was a lifelong friend. He came when the cavalry called.

You have to understand something, Jack is/was a very wealthy man. I say this because I have learned that wealth cannot be defined by money. Although it took a lot of capital, Jack should be considered wealthy because of his ability to continue to learn, coupled by his compulsion for preparation and survival. And as I am finding out, friends in very low places.

This stuff only happened in movies, not in real life, at least not my life. I never tried hacking anyone's computer, never met with a foreign diplomat, never ran for public office, never won the lottery, this has more implications than I thought. The more I thought about it, the more I was convinced that OUR right to Free Speech was being trampled on by Citizens United. Since the Supreme Court decided money was speech, those with the most money wanted everyone to just sit down, shut up and take it. Do not forget, this is the same Big Money pool that funded politicians for immediate voter suppression in the Bible Belt states.

Well, you can go to your grave knowing you were right Plumb, I thought. You can also take satisfaction in knowing this all could have been prevented. Ask yourself one question, why would Republicans go to such great lengths, spend so much money enacting voter suppression laws that mostly restrict those that would vote Democratic?

The answer is very simple. Democrats outnumber Republicans and control of Congress and the Senate both would be in the hands of the Democrats. Big money cannot allow this, because Democrats want to use government for the benefit of the people. Republicans want to use government to rape the middle class and expand the already gross income inequality that exist currently in this country. Thats is the nerve center at which Republicans are driven.

In Texas, the last presidential election showed that only 4% of the eligible 39% Latino vote went to the polls and had their voices heard. Imagine the political makeup of Texas if the apathy in the Hispanic community were to vanish and they actually casted a ballot for who they wanted representing them?

Arizona has one of the most eyebrow raising situations that exist in politics. The majority of voters are concentrated in the county of the Capitol city, Phoenix. Phoenix is in Maricopa County, where there are four million voters roughly. The Latino and Black vote represent roughly 1.5 million of those votes. During the last midterm elections, the congressional representative, Trent Franks(R), received little over 800,000 votes, while the vote from the Latino and Black vote went vastly underrepresented. That could have been one less vote on the side of Republicans, and a vote for democracy in Congress. Remember, Rep. Franks is one of the unanimous Republican votes in Congress that voted over fifty times to defund the Affordable Healthcare Act and make sure millions of working Americans did not have the right to affordable and quality healthcare. That is where the power of the people needs to be exercised more than ever.

The sheriff of Maricopa County, Joe Arpiao(R), is the big mystery to me. He has cost the taxpayers of Maricopa County hundreds of millions of dollars in lawsuits from his illegal behavior on racial profiling to inmate deaths while under the care of his custody. He spends taxpayer dollars on personal projects that have nothing to do with county business, and is one of the most self serving people in existence. In the last election, Arpiao received just over 670,000 votes, his Democratic opponent only lost by 80,000 votes. These are perfect examples, nationwide, that show how important the vote is, and more importantly that the votes are there! If getting rid of a racist like Joe is not enough to go to the polls, then we are all truly doomed!

All of these thoughts combined with major a migraine made me think of one thing, where are those damn pills? I grabbed what was needed, probably a little above the recommended dosage but after that experience I really needed something to put me on my ass. I drifted off to sleep filled with questions.

XI

Instead of staying in my home for the next two weeks like a caged rat, I thought it would be in the best interest of my family to continue my life like nothing had happened for the time being. I begged them to stay home, but tried to do so without divulging too much information because well the house is bugged… Laurie and Gabby being the stubborn independent women that they are refused. I knew this is one battle that I can never win. I did mention, very indirectly, that if they did happen to go anywhere, to make sure they did so in a very public place.

I arrived at the University and tried to remain as casual and normal as someone who is being watched by the United States Government can be. John was right, reporters were waiting for me outside my classroom. I refused to comment on anything, plenty of comments were asked about how I got to look like this. I ignored the question and offered the opportunity to sit in on one of my Think Tanks if they would like. I knew things would be less than thrilling so it felt innocuous inviting them in. Plus, with reporters around no one would dare try anything with that caliber of witness around. All I would ask of them is that they remain respectful to my students during the class. I walked down the steps, amidst whispers and conversations about my health, and stopped at the Chalkboard to write something on the board "E Pluribus Unum". Who can tell me what this means? "One of many" came from a voice that sounded vaguely familiar from the back of the class. Correct, I said as I scoured the class to find the voice that knew the answer my cursive search around the room gave no hint as to the owner of that voice. By the time I swung my head to the far right of the room all I saw was the back of a figure, which looked like that of a man, being erased by the door that closed behind him.

For the next two weeks Think Tanks basically went this way, there was open forum but to an extent. I had one half of the class administer bullying on the other side, all the while teaching when it occurs and how to identify it. Not only that but we thought of ways that we could defeat it. How when engaged in an open forum with another individual or organization that uses such tactics as bullying and how to overcome them. How to still get your point across, and ultimately the best tactic we found to eliminate bullying is to expose them for what they are. Taking the offensive, unlike my plan, and exposing the playbook of your opponent catching him off guard. Either your opposition will continue down their plan of attack, allowing you to be seen as clever, calculating and insightful, or they will be forced to change their tactics unless they plan to leave themselves vulnerable to ridicule (or wind up in the emergency room).

I figured, hoped, that this style of teaching would not arouse suspicion since it would not conflict with my views and opinions on the corruption that was Republican controlled politics. Engaging students to process topics on their own, without my input, was a good measure for me anyway to determine just where the class felt as far as the current political gridlock that was Washington D.C., and how historically it measures with previous civilizations successes and failures.

Mr. Agent and his following did not even try to hide anymore. I saw that uniform dark suit, sunglasses and stoic glare on their faces as I conducted business on campus. It was third and long for me, fear was their blitz package, the play clock was running and it was obvious that intimidation was supposed to put me in line. Of course fear was not the emotion that was channeling my thoughts and decisions, it was anger and survival. The fact that I had a guardian angel out there somewhere was a little comforting. Very little since there was just one of him, that I knew of anyway. This waiting game, with the safety of Laurie and Gabby now within the crosshairs, was going to give me an ulcer.

After a thinktank one evening about two weeks to the date, I heard from John.

XII

Good thing I was sitting down. Going through a stack of composition books, I saw one with the name "John" in huge capital letters on the outside cover. Naturally I opened it hastily, and the first line said, "Close this book! Take it home and read it in your safe room where we met." I closed it right away, put it in my laptop bag, grabbed my keys, and headed out the door for home. I guess Mr. Agent should have thought about being more discreet, now that I knew I was being followed I strolled my normal pace to not give away any excitement in my chest. With my head looking downward as if in defeat, I acted on auto-pilot and tried to emit the vibe I had been beaten. I drove the speed limit or just under so I would not show any rush to get home for something. "Just be cool Plumb" I kept telling myself, but inside I was like a schoolgirl, giddy with a note to read when she got home. A secret just for two, but in this case a lot more than a schoolyard crush was on the line.

When I arrived home, I used the garage door opener to park the car in the garage, and immediately closed it when I was fully in, the engine was still running for Christ sake. I turned the car off,exited the vehicle and went straight to the "safe room". I cannot believe I am calling my downstairs bathroom a safe room now, what has the world come to. I am not spy material. In my haste I had totally forgotten that there was a bomb shelter just for these type of situations but that is besides the point. I opened up the letter and on the inside it read this:

Hello Professor Plumb,

If you are reading this then that means that you have been selected. Your mission if you choose to accept is to join the growing movement upon Zipporah. Your agent that is assigned to you will inform you on the next steps necessary to begin your move to Zipporah. You are allowed to bring two family members as long as they are of opposite sex,-

I couldn't help thinking to myself, what is this Mission Impossible, and wait two people... There has to be a mistake. What was going on? I have the Republican led goon squad after me, I send a silly subliminal message that only one person on the planet would know, now I get this mysterious message that is for "my eyes only", this was way too cloak and dagger for an old man like me.

this is the only stipulation. We are accumulating some of the greatest minds this world has ever been blessed with having, consider it an honor for being selected. I urge that you follow these instructions and listen to the voice of reason. There are powers at play that you cannot understand. Please heed this warning.
"The proof is in the pudding"

There is only one man that would ever use that saying... It had to be, but could it be? Could it be Jack. Long ago we agreed a saying, that we would say if we ever needed assistance from control from a power that had grown to big and corrupt to govern. And this was that exact moment. It was then that I realized this had been Jack's play all along. I don't understand why he had to rough me up so much, I suppose I am not the only one that got selected and the process was probably built upon fear. How was he supposed to know that the CIA has become involved and was trying to condemn me as traitor of the state. I really think that the press , conference had reached him, had done some good.

I read the instructions. twice. In the morning I would ask Laurie and Gabby to follow me to look at something, I had questions. The reality was that we were going to play "Get Smart" and use the bathroom as the "cone of silence". Time to unveil to them that their lives would change forever. That there would be no more life as they knew it, but a change, a new life that would be different from what they are used to and the possibility for a peaceful existence was possible. That would be an easy sell for the man that ruled his castle by the motto of " do it my way or else", but I did not live with women made to dance to that tune. Laurie and Gabby were reasonable, but when it is time to run for your life, having one captain at the rudder is definitely the man for the job. And I would have to sell them most convincingly.

I left the instructions in the cone of silence, and went upstairs to go to bed wondering if it would be the last night I would have in it. I layed down thinking about just who exactly was responsible for the events that lead up to this time in my life. Who in Congress wanted me there, and in the shape and condition to be scared out of my wits to not make waves and be a "good boy". Most importantly, which group of Billionaires and Millionaires wanted me out of the way, that list was powerful and had the resources to make it happen. Could it be the Oil and Gas industry, Defense Contractors, or ex-Congressmen/women, that get $100,000+ per year and free medical paid for by the taxpayers? (after that stunt of a graduation speech) Maybe they were all in on it together, "now you are getting paranoid Plumb", I thought. Go to sleep. It would not be that easy. Pretty much all I thought about was that these bastards were going to silence me, continue their destruction of America, and the planet with not only the threat of going back to war in the Middle East, Iran initially, on a path to nuclear destruction, but the refusal to accept climate change is real, and significantly contributed to mankind's carbon imprint to our atmosphere. I had the weirdest dream that night.

I dreamed that I was in Oslo, Norway to receive the Nobel Peace Prize on solving the problems the reduction of carbon emissions on the planet. My idea of eliminating totally the internal combustion engine. No more would mankind pump carbon emissions into the atmosphere due to the necessity of reliable transportation to get back and forth to work, and other necessary functions people need to get where they need to go.

Ladies, Gentleman, Distinguished colleagues, and my fellow brothers and sisters in Christ around the globe. Thank you for the opportunity to be here before you today, humble and stunned that someone like me would ever be thought of on such an esteemed level with people that have brought about serious change for the benefit of humankind. It just seemed like such an easy fix to the issue of Global Warming. Solar energy has been developed and proven to be a free source of energy, that can be stored and harnessed in battery reservoirs to such a degree that sufficient power exist even during times when you are traveling when the sun is warming the other side of the globe. It was time to build manufacturing plants, run on solar energy, manufacturing solar powered cars. This put Americans around the United States and citizens of other countries worldwide, to work, making a living, churning the economies of the global markets. It gave mankind a universal project, creating the opportunity for people around the globe to set aside differences and make the change needed to lay to rest the dinosaur that is the Oil and Gas industry, leaving our resources in the earth where they belong because mining for them has a huge carbon footprint on our planet.

Our species has evolved and made significant improvements in our society to improve the quality of our lives. Saving our species by turning our collective voices is why this change was possible. In the United States, people became frustrated by the gridlock that was Washington D.C. Democrats fighting for reform over tax laws that gave the "Sheriff of Nottingham" the right to give all the tax breaks to the rich, and put the burden of funding the government on the middle and impoverished classes. The rich got Richer, and the rest got poorer, mostly due to the Oil and Gas industries. Republicans wanted to continue down the path that led to the fall of the Roman Empire. Only by the power of the people did this finally have a chance to happen. They voted out Republicans, enacted laws that kept lobbyist off the grounds of the Capitol Building, and put the interest of the people over the interest of the rich.

I woke in a deep sweat, chest heaving for air. Was there anyone in my bedroom this evening? Thank God Laurie is the soundest sleeper in the world. Thank God that was just a dream, "you are such an egomaniac Plumb" I thought. I was glad at least that Bernie Sanders was saying the things I believe to be true, there really does need to be a revolution. Peaceful, at the ballot box, finally, just let the people decide how best they want to be represented.

There was no way I was going back to sleep, my pillow was wet with perspiration and so was my side of the bed (yes, it was just sweat). My t-shirt was soaked and I knew a shower was in order. It was 3:23am, but first I went to check on Gabby to make sure she was ok. I stuck my head in her room, found her safely in dreamland and went downstairs to make sure all the hatches were still battoned. Good, no spooks lurking about, I went upstairs, grabbed clean underwear and t-shirt, and washed the scariness, that was my sleep, off my body. That hot shower felt great, it relaxed me, I felt fresh, the house would be mine to enjoy before anyone woke up. First I would make a pot of coffee, then make some toast and peel a banana. I love the peace and quiet. This would afford me the time to pack a bag, gather my toiletry items and help with Laurie and Gabby getting their things ready.

So much for peace and quiet, so much for coffee for that matter! John was sitting at the island counter in the kitchen holding his index finger to his lips, signaling for me to be quiet. I just put my head down and headed for the bathroom.

John didn't say much to me, while I was in the bathroom I closed the door and thought to myself "What the hell is this man doing in my house, AGAIN. And more importantly how the hell did he get in? All the doors were locked I checked them myself." While I leaned and looked at myself in the mirror trying to solve these complex world problems I heard a faint knock on the door. Followed by a whisper "It's Time" John said, Time for what I thought?! Ok Plumb, gather yourself kiddo, I pulled myself together and came to the door. I opened it and sure enough John was gone, but God Forbid there was another letter on the floor where I am sure he was standing. This one was different, it had a red wax seal and no heading on the front. I felt an overwhelming watching presence, but before I could open it I had to check that my family was ok. Where had this mad man gone. I checked both Laurie and Gabby's room and they were both fine and completely safe. Was I really becoming that paranoid, I checked every inch of the house until finally I came across it. There was a window open, the draft hit me in the face immediately alerting me to where John must have made his escape. This window was on the second floor, it was at the very least a 20ft drop from here to the ground. This man was insane, of course he left a little note himself the cheeky bastard. I opened it and a pamphlet for Charlotte Amtrak fell out to the ground. I picked it up and read the note inside, it had one word on it "Run!"

XIII

I ran instantly down the stairs down to the basement to the safe room. I took a knife and frantically opened the Letter. To my surprise it opened rather easily. Inside it was another letter, but this one was different...

Hello my friend,

*I know that things right now might seem a little hectic but believe me the guild, or probably how you know them now as John, have you and your family's best interest at heart. They will probably screen this letter to make sure that I am not alerting you or tipping you off about anything but believe me, you arrogant over protective assholes my friend Plumb is on the righteous side. Noah, I am sure you are aware of what is happening in the world. We believe that there is going to be a catastrophic event, something of such a high magnitude that we could be witnessing within our lifetime **Human Extinction.** I implore you to follow these next steps carefully and help insure the safety and security of your family. I know the last letter that these Assholes sent you told you that you would ultimately have to choose when it came to whom you brought with you to Zipporah. But I am here to tell you that you can bring your whole family, they will always have a place here on Zipporah. I mean for Christ sakes, I am the one that made it. I am sure that you got the pamphlets for the train station, go there immediately. Wake up your family, gather what belongings you can without raising any suspicion and get your family into your car. After this head to said Train station and await your next message.*

I stood frozen for a second, for fear that my knees would give way and I would fall flat on my face. But that protective instinct engaged in my brain, and getting Laurie and Gabby to safety was the only priority that existed. First thing to do was get myself together. I grabbed my duffel bag, put in a week's worth of underwear, socks and t-shirts. I rolled my favorite hoodie, and put it in the duffel, along with deodorant, toothbrush and toothpaste. My huge bottle of tylenol, a razor and aftershave were the last things i threw in. I tiptoed down the stairs and placed my bag by the garage door. Laurie would be next, I closed the bedroom door before I turned the light on, to prevent any illumination from alerting Gabby before it was absolutely necessary, and flipped the switch. Laurie immediately rolled over, squinted her eyes and asked, "what time is it?" I told her, "that is not important", I walked to the side of the bed where she was and whispered, "do you remember what we talked about in the emergency room waiting area?" She bolted upright and threw the covers off of her. "Gabby is fine, just shower, pack a bag and lets go. I will get Gabby."

That daughter of mine, time and time again I forget how sensitive her other senses are since she does have the gift of hearing. She was sitting up in her bed and just asked in plain english (ASL), is it time to go daddy? Shower and pack your bag, we are leaving, is all I needed to reply back to her. She motioned for me to get out of her room, and I smiled, gave her the "I love you" sign, and closed her door.

The note said, "run", I got that, but what I did not want to do was to cause them to panic and forget anything that might be important. Inside I was screaming like I was in a real life horror movie, and I was the girl. When I went back into my bedroom, laurie was finishing up in the shower,I actually thought to myself that this might be the last time I get to see my wife naked and try and take advantage of that, I know James Bond would but as fate would have it my last name is Plumber, so no end of the world spy "laying down pipe" sex for me. She kicked me out of the bedroom and told me to wait downstairs, "real smooth Plumb" I thought. Make yourself useful and put your bag in the back of the car, I told myself. That nagging question kept popping up in my head, "who wants me dead?", I just hoped that the one hundred mile drive going southwest to Charlotte would put distance and trouble behind me. After my bag was in the car, I went inside to my office and grabbed my stash of mad money, $1500, and put it in my pocket. Using debit or credit cards would leave a trace and we would have to stay under the radar as much as possible. Within ten minutes, my girls were dressed, packed and downstairs. "That was fast" I said. Gabby cocked her head, pursed her lips a little and signed, "we have been ready since that night at the hospital". "Where are we Going?" I signed back to her, "not here, let's get in the car".

We had one last look around the house, I thought to myself, "Credit Bureau be damned", we were leaving for good, witness protection if you think of it that way, from the government. I got excited a little for a chance at a fresh start in life, smiled and turned to Laurie. "Come on baby", I told her, "time for a new life". She grumbled, "I kinda liked this one". "But I support you so I go where you go, let's go." We made sure all the lights were out in the house, the alarm was set, just to show we were coming back, left our cell phones on the kitchen counter and closed the door from the washroom into the garage. I made sure I got in first and Laurie and Gabby were far away when I started the car. You could say I had spy movie paranoia. I made sure everyone was in the car and seat belts. It was still dark outside when I opened the garage door,so I left the lights out on the car as long as it took to get to the street. The gas tank was already full so we would not have to stop along the way and that was good. "Run" does not mean stop for breakfast along the way. Good thing while I was waiting when they were in the shower, to take the liberty of packing some snacks in our mini-cooler with a freezer pack. "How much money do you have?" Laurie asked me. $1500 I told her, she said, "give it to me". I handed her my stash, and she laughed, "I had $3000". So now armed with $4500 cash on hand, we rolled toward the onramp we usually used to get to Interstate 85. It was a short drive, and in just a few minutes we were driving westbound on Interstate 85. So far so good I thought to myself. I dared not say anything to jinx the good fortune we started out with. The sun was beginning to creep over the horizon in my rear view mirror, and my vision was impaired to the point that it physically hurt to look into the rearview or side mirrors. I leaned my head to escape the glare and told myself I could put up with a few minutes of leaning while driving, just long enough for the sun to rise out of its glaring reflection angle that was totally unforgiving. Mother Nature had me in a blind spot for the next twenty minutes, which to my string of luck lately was par for the course, because after about ten minutes my neck started to tense and I felt a good headache gathering the resources to start this trip off with a bang. I had no choice but to sit upright and tolerate the sun as best as possible, so I focused on the striped white lines on the road to keep the sun's glare out of my direct path of vision.

That seemed to work, the headache was thwarted, for now. Slowly the sun rose to ease my field of vision, it looked like it had the possibilities to be a great day. The sky was blue, there were light patches of brilliant white puffy clouds where you had the opportunity to play the "what shape does that cloud look like" game. The day became progressively brighter, and one by one, the cars behind and in front of us began turning off their headlights. I thought the best way to travel would be to obey all the rules of the road,so I stayed in the number two lane as much as possible with the cruise set to the speed limit, I was not going to attract any undue attention to myself, keep the mood as light as possible and the most important thing, **do not drink anything before you get to the train station**. The last thing i wanted was to stop because of a full bladder and give anyone the chance to prevent us from getting to our destination. Traffic was easy this early, it was getting to be around 7:30am, and by my calculation the trip should take approximately two hours, barring any traffic slow downs. When I was able to look into the rearview mirror without burning my retinas, I noticed a State Trooper behind us in the number one lane. The trooper was about five car lengths behind me. And it stayed there until we neared the city of Burlington.

I admit, I felt relief when I saw the trooper exit the Interstate around that city, I was also glad I did not say anything to Laurie or Gabby. I did not want them turning around and giving the trooper anything suspicious, "act normal Plumb" was the recurring theme that kept running through my mind. Approaching Greensboro, I pondered, then we will be about half way there and then it will be time to say goodbye to this car. I had to make sure there was nothing left in here in case anyone decided to search it after we were gone. I would lock it, take the keys and drop them in a trash receptacle somewhere along the way, a dumpster would be an ideal spot to throw keys, that is where no one would think to look for car keys.

That thought process dissipated quickly when I saw another State Trooper parked along the divider between the west and eastbound lanes. As we drove by, the trooper pulled out from spot where he/she was parked, and started westbound on Interstate 85, towards Greensboro. This time Laurie noticed and asked what my speed was. I told her the cruise was set at the speed limit, and she said, "ok, I just saw that trooper pull out when we passed, just want to make sure its not coming for us". "It shouldn't be", I replied, "we are not speeding, our registration is current and there is no safety issues that we have with this car". She leaned over, looked at the speedometer, leaned back, shrugged her shoulders and gave an "ok" look at me. I felt better knowing I was not in the wrong on anything here, but the tension had obviously risen within Laurie. It sure felt like we were being followed.

Then I saw something, a shadow of what appeared to be an aircraft overhead. The sun had turned into an ally, and shown the shadowed reflection of what ultimately turned out to be, a drone. Laurie kept looking in the side mirror on the passenger side to see if the trooper was still following. I could tell because I was doing the same thing. Again, I never alerted her about the drone following overhead. Keeping their blood pressure down was important to me.

I finally had to apply the brakes and disconnect the cruise control due to road construction. This significantly extended our time on the road because there were orange barrels along the interstate until Graham, NC. The trooper following us pulled over again in the median dividing east from westbound lanes without a State Trooper escort. "Jesus! Stop being so paranoid Plumb!" I thought to myself, I let myself relax a little thinking that we escaped before anyone left the house and John had saved us, but that drone image kept popping up in my head to counterbalance what sanity I had left to work with. Laurie placed her hand on my knee and started rubbing that joint. It felt great, and I exhaled just knowing she was there. I never could fool her on what my emotions truly were.

From Graham to Whitsett, I was able to re-engage the cruise control and start making some of that lost time back. Once we reached Guilford County lines, the speed limit dropped to sixty five miles per hour. Every other mile or so was either a State trooper, county sheriff, City of Greensboro Police or any other various small incorporated city located within County lines. At one point all I could do was chuckle once again allowing the thought that of all this was on my behalf, at least so far none of them decided to pull in behind us and illuminate the emergency lights on their vehicles. That drone was a while ago,and although i did not spot another glimpse of another, that did not mean that they were not still there. I needed a joint!

From Salisbury to Charlotte, there was a law enforcement vehicle posted at every onramp overpass. Even if I wanted to take a piss, there was no way I could do so without seeing some type of cop somewhere. Thank God Laurie nor Gabby mentioned the word bathroom, and I was not about to put it on anyone's mind. When we transitioned to Interstate 77, police vehicles almost caused an accident behind us trying to stay behind us through the interchange.

All I got was a damned pamphlet to the AmTrak Station in Charlotte, what was I supposed to do when i got there? It was obvious, they were definitely monitoring our movements. If I even tried to go to will call, I had no idea what the plan was after we got to the train station, if we got to train station. There were police cars at every exit along this stretch of the interstate. These guys knew how to tell if you were trying to escape. Why drive to Charlotte to get on a train when there was an AmTrak right there in Durham?

I was just a pawn in their game, collateral damage as it were, how was I going get out of my car, get to a terminal, without being stopped. I prayed John had a very good plan. As it turned out, he did. A few hundred yards prior to getting off on the Graham exit, a Police vehicle pulled in behind us and turned on his emergency lights. Who do I see get out of the police car, John. Behind sunglasses that made his eyes mirrors to those that looked into them, he strolled to the driver side door and leaned in. "Laurie, Gabby, I wish this were better circumstances to meet in, but I need you to come with me right now." "Professor, get off at this exit, turn right and go to Tenth Street. There on the corner you will find a black Chevy Impala with Florida plates on it. There will be a room key for the Day's Inn on 9th Street in between North Church Street and North Tryon Street. Do not leave the key to his vehicle in close proximity when you ditch this vehicle." I looked at both my girls and said, "go with him, I trust him, I promise to see you soon." I kissed Laurie, John gritted his teeth and said, "Now!" Then, "Please" in a much calmer voice. "If you come with me now you have a much better chance of seeing him again". The police car in front of us put it in reverse and sped backward along the shoulder with his emergency lights on, trying desperately to get to our spot. Simultaneously, Laurie and Gabby jumped out of the car and ran back to John's police car. "Go!" John yelled, and I did not hesitate. Good thing I said my Rosary that morning, because I had to get some good luck going my way. I threw the gear shift into drive and turned the wheel left to avoid colliding with the police car coming my way, fast!

No cars were approaching in the slow lane, so I stomped on the accelerator, and swung out into traffic. I looked into my rearview mirror, and saw flashing emergency lights headed our way, southbound on 77. I had time to get to Impala and get away before he could slow down to exit, and try to follow where I went. And when my car was found I would be long gone. After I passed the police car, he stopped his car, opened his door, removed his service weapon and fired two rounds through the rear window in my car. As the bullets passed by, a piece of glass that was flying past me, cut the right side of my cheek. Mostly it just stung, but DAMN, what a sting.

John un holstered his weapon and fired one round at the trooper, hitting him in the unprotected part of the back of his right shoulder that his vest did not cover. The officer dropped his weapon and collapsed along the open driver's side of his police vehicle. John pivoted an "about face", fired one round through the front windshield of the oncoming police car causing it to swerve right into the guardrail, decommissioning that cop car. I saw John run back to his vehicle, but never saw the results of the ensuing gunfire that was happening in my six o'clock. I hoped the decision letting Laurie and Gabby go with John was a good idea, then I thought, they were shooting at me after they got out of the car, maybe the girls were not the target after all and would be safe, that was my prayer anyway. As I was exiting the Interstate, I saw John pulling away from the shoulder onto the southbound lane closest to the shoulder. I exited Graham, and turned left onto 10th Street, sure enough, just as John said, there was the black Impala. I parked directly behind it, exited my car, locked it and headed for the Chevy.

The Impala was unlocked, I got in the driver's seat, found the keys in the ignition and turned the car on. As I pulled away from the curb to get away from the area, the sounds of sirens approaching were rapidly increasing and I could see the pulsating strobe of intermittent blue lights reflecting off parked cars and business windows. From nowhere, a voice came over the speakers in the car, "continue along this road until North Poplar Street, then turn right". I was about five hundred feet away from my car when I saw the first police unit. It continued along Graham toward the freeway, and I was grateful for another break. Just a few seconds later, a police car pulled in behind my car, the one I am abandoning. I turned right onto North Poplar and continued to follow the directions to the motel. Along the way to the motel, Police Car after police car continued along the street, sirens blaring. I was lucky that John had selected such a dark tinted window vehicle. I was moving completely incognito. At one point I saw a police chopper heading behind me in the direction I just left. I continued on the road until I reached the motel. I waited for a few minutes to make sure that I wasn't being followed, the police sirens began to fade as they moved farther away and I knew it was now safe. Damnit, I thought to myself, now what.

As I sat there I couldn't help but noticing a gentleman from the hotel walking up to my car. No, I thought, please don't let him come here. For the love of God, go away but he didn't listen neither did God apparently. He reached my car window and knocked three times, I contemplated waiting for him to go away, but I noticed that his name Tag said John. This wasn't the same man that I had seen earlier, but he walked with such a certain militaristic movement that made me think he had to be military trained. I rolled down my window very hesitantly, only half way. Before I could even get any words out he said, "Mr Plumb your room is ready, John informed us of your arrival. Here is your room key." Before I could even say anything John had handed me the card and had begun to walk away. All I could do now is follow my room card, the room 13:3. Keep my mouth shut got it John, guys weren't messing around. I started the strategic walk to my room, I checked the map on the first floor and found my room. Of course it was on the second floor, of course. I walked up the stairs and took a right. I rounded the corner and came up to my door. The lights were off inside, I took out my key and put it in the lock. I heard the locks turn and the door open. I looked around to make sure the coast was clear, which of course it was and went inside. I looked around the room. It was rather normal, single bed, Pillow, alarm clock, lamp on a bedstand and a rabbit ear TV. One thing was very odd though, the water was running. I was inside by this point when I had heard the water stop. I tried to move out of the way to try and find a weapon to defend myself to the best of my ability but it was too late. Before I could even get to what I would think would be a weapon in this instance a lamp, a woman had come out of the bathroom locking eyes with me, a gun pointed in my direction.

I stopped dead in my tracks, who was this I thought. Once again before I could even ask questions she started talking. "My name is John, please take a seat." Seriously another John, now it had hit me that the John's were the good guys, the Guild. I sat down on the bed and said "How can I help you John?" at this time she had lowered the gun and started to reach into her pocket. She pulled out an envelope and handed it to me, I had no idea what was inside, all that it read on the front was NCDOT, the only thing I could think of was North Carolina Public Transit. "You want me to take a bus?!" I exclaimed, "Yes" she said. "And we would like to put you in a disguise Mr.Plumb". I looked at her, raised an eyebrow and asked, "what kind of disguise?" A huge grin appeared on her face as she reached her arm into the bathroom, then pulled out a dress that looked like a belonged in a quilting bee. "No way you are getting me in a dress", I said. she picked up the television remote control from the sink countertop,pointed it at the television and turned it on. There for God and all to see, was my picture on the tube. The reporter was saying that

I was wanted for the shooting of a police officer on Interstate 77. The officer, who they refused to identify, was in the hospital in stable condition, and a second shooting, striking another police car, causing it to crash, no injuries reported. She turned the television off, and stared at me, enough said.

"This must be very troubling for you professor", she said, "look inside the envelope, there is something special just for you." I opened the envelope, saw my bus pass, boarding pass for my AmTrak departure, and a joint! "With everything that is going on, I am sure you could use some time to exhale, no pun intended". "This strain was named after you professor, it is called Numb Plumb, for the cerebral man." I thought there is a God afterall, and he loves me. then she walked past me, grabbed her cross body bag, reached in and pulled out a wad of cash. "We told laurie you might need your cash back since you are traveling separately. "Why separate us?" I asked. "The fastest way to travel is alone, and time is of the essence," she replied. And the Numb Plumb will make your transition into my grandmother much smoother. (Fire when ready Plumb!) I sparked up and took a huge inhale, I wanted to get the full effects of Numb Plumb as quickly as possible. Once I started smoking John immediately got to work, she pulled out a kit from underneath the bed and put it next to me on the bed. She began to remove all kinds of makeup supplies. I didn't mind, I had a fantastic Joint and my mind was starting to race. This stuff really had a cerebral touch, just as I was sitting there thinking to myself the situation that I had gotten myself in I started making some epiphanies.

All of a sudden I realized why they had gotten me high, they wanted me to be cooperative, to be spaced out if you will. They wanted to me act like a grandma, truly an old lady. Well, they have been right about everything else so far, and now seeing that I am wanted for attempted homicide on the cop I was not left with much of a choice. After making all of these connections while John was finishing up my hair and make-up, the wig that she had put on me was really itchy, I consciously decided to cooperate. John said, "Ok Mr. Plumb I am done with you hair and makeup, if you could just put on this dress we can get you on your way".

I think I had gone a little too far with that joint because I was completely iced, I couldn't move. I tried to say something, but then decided I would just relax and enjoy some relaxing after what just happened. Numb Plumb had really made me numb, John eagerly waited for my reply, when nothing came out of my mouth, not even a simple gesture she became a little agitated. She said, "Looks like I am going to do this myself, don't worry Mr. Plumb that strain will start to come down here in the next 15 minutes and then you will be sitting really pretty. We just have to get you in this dress and on your way, please sit still. Finally I was able to at least know, something I had been trying to do for the last 10 minutes. This high was amazing. John began to put the dress on me, of course she had to undress me first...Forgive me Laurie for when your read this, there was nothing that I could really do.

She finished dressing me, she reached down and handed me a blue purse. "Here" she said, "this will complete the look, can you grab it?" It felt as though I was fighting against my own body to try and grip this maybe 5lb hand bag. Finally I was able to clench my hand together and grasp the handbag. She then began to help me up off of the bed, and it felt like the most exacerbated process in the world. John grabbed me up underneath her arm and began to help me to the door. She had me under her arm when she noticed that I had left the envelope on the bed. In my defense, it had been so long since I had smoked a joint, the effects were telling. She leaned me up against the wall next to the boob tube and walked over to the bed to retrieve it. She came back to me with the envelope and placed it in the purse that she had given me. I laughed on the inside, but again no outer expression. She told me when we reached the door, "Ok, Mr. Plumb after we leave this door you are completely on your own. Proceed at your own risk, don't forget the envelope. Here is a cane, use it to help and stabilize yourself".

I took the cane from her, "Goodbye and good luck Mr. Plumb. And oh the bus stop is about 500ft from the hotel entrance". With that she closed the door and I had basically been thrown outside. I gathered myself, thank god they didn't change my shoes. There would have been no way in hell that I could have done this in heels, I don't understand how women walk in them now. Or why for that matter. Crazy how the high heel shoe was invented in Europe during the 16th Century. European royalty would actually wear these shoes, men too, to make themselves feel and seem larger than life...Focus Plumb, god this was some good shit. I took my cane in hand and used it to regain my control of my stiff and swaying body. I started to walk towards the stairs, the whole time I felt as though I was having a conversation with my body. Ok, left foot now right foot. I could not help but have that song from the animated classic, "Santa Claus is comin to town". One foot in front of the other. It played the whole time while I was walking to the stairs, god if I hadn't remembered that song at that moment I don't think I would have ever even made it to the stairs. Once I had reached the stairs, which at this point had started to look less like Mount Everest, had that much time really passed from the door to the stairs.

I could not believe how euphoric this high was, I felt great, I did not even care that I had traveled this distance in such a long amount of time. I started to walk down the stairs, the best comparison I can think of is a deer on ice...I looked like a deer on ice. After another 15 minutes, now I was beginning to realise how perfect this costume was. A woman that looked the way I did walking down these stairs would be taking about the same amount of time anyways, it was genius, at this point I completely played into the costume and the game for that matter. I saw the entrance of the hotel to my right along with the bus stop just like John had said. I started my jaunt to the bus stop, which felt less like a jaunt and more like a 10k.

At the bus stop, there were two other individuals waiting for the bus. A mom, I want to say in her twenties and her 5 year old son. I began to talk to them, I thought why not we have some time. "Hello, my name is Pro...(I caught myself I had totally forgotten I was dressed as a woman, I changed the tone of my voice and proceeded) *Cough* *cough* Hi, my name is Patrise sorry about that, once you get old hunny everything starts to go downhill. Even your voice apparently. How are you two doing today?" The woman turned and looked at me with a smile on her face, she was happy to converse with another human being. "Hi", she said, "My name is Stephanie, this is my daughter Gretchen". "Why hello I said, it is a pleasure to meet both of you."

We conversed about our lives, women love to gossip I thought, so talk, be a sociable old woman. She told me they were trying to leave an abusive relationship, and since Daddy Dearest was passed out on the sofa after another fifth of Canadian Club whiskey, she had enough and was not going to raise a child to learn to accept abuse and disrespect. I admired her for that. She was going to the train station and headed for Las Vegas, New Mexico, and stay with an old friend she was recently reaquainted with thanks to Facebook. All she needed to do was safely make it the remaining ten blocks or so it took to get there, then they could start a new life together where love abounds plentiful in their home. "You should write poetry" I told her, "you have a loving aura around you". "That is funny", she said, "I have always wanted to write. Now I have the pain with which to draw on for a source of inspiration". That almost brought a tear to my eye, how some people have to suffer so much so that others can enjoy the depths of the messages they suffered through to gain such insight is awe inspiring.

I began to get my bearings a little better, but still enjoyed the effects of the Numb Plumb. Here we both sat, like ducks in a barrell, hoping no one would decide to come our way and disturb the peace that was the night. In the distance, the marquis atop the front of the bus was lit along with the headlights, our escape was coming and I was very grateful to be getting mobile instead of sitting and waiting. Getting to where Laurie and Gabby were was of paramount importance. But where were they? My stomach began to ball up and anger was fueling the tension when I let myself worry about their whereabouts. I thought that there was no way I would ever spend $1500 from here to where ever I was going, so I handed $500 to Stephanie. "You need this more than I do", I told her. Her bottom lip started quivering and the floodgate of tears began streaming down her face, "Thank you so much", she said, "All we have is our tickets at will call." I said, "The Lord gave me five loaves and two fishes, what else am I supposed to do with this?"

She leapt at me and threw her arms around me, at once she could tell I was no old woman. She let go and looked at me with surprise. I said, "You are not the only one leaving a "bad situation", "I promise I am one of the good guys". Her look was not encouraging, so I said, "Witness Protection, kind of". I tried easing her mind, that I have never hurt anyone, I have not fired a weapon in twenty years, and I was being framed for a crime I did not commit. That I was trying to get to my wife and daughter, and I would do everything in my power to make sure they got to the train station so they could start this new chapter of their lives as well.

"Well I am sure you have no intention of harming us or doing us ill will,or you would not have been so generous with your gift to us". "Exactly", I said,"not all men are monsters".

Just then, before the bus could take us out of here, a red Ford Thunderbird, with its tires squealing around the corner,came toward us. "Its him!" she screamed. Stephanie grabbed her daughter tightly and started screaming,"Leave us alone!" I almost laughed when I saw what came out of the car. This skinny, mullet headed, stained wife beater shirt wearing, loud mouth came stumbling out of the car. He got brave when he saw me, must have thought I was a defenseless old lady because he yelled at me, "Stay in your seat grandma, this don't concern you!" He was twenty feet away and I thought I was going to vomit right there from the stench of his alcohol vomit soaked shirt. I thought to myself, I will stay right here and use the element of surprise to clock his ass. "Do not move" I mumbled to Stephanie,

"I got this". With all his bravado showing for what he thought was an easy prey, he walked past me and reached for Stephanie's arm. I reached over and grabbed his wrist as hard as I could, continued his momentum toward the bench, then stood, used my right hand, grabbed him from behind his head and let his own momentum crash his face into to bus stop bench. Baby Daddy hit the ground like a bag of lead falling from his 5'5" height. Where did that come from Plumb, I thought. "Let's go!" Stephanie shouted,she was in the driver's seat of the Thunderbird before I knew what was going on. We had a better mode of transportation now to get us to the AmTrak.

XIV

I started toward the Thunderbird, still feeling a little woozy from the Numb Plumb, plus that little spin move coming off the bench, my steps were not the most agile. My left foot caught an incline in the sidewalk cement, and I tripped, causing my right foot to have to step longer than usual to stop my momentum from carrying me face first into the sidewalk. It was not easy stopping myself from falling, and I was able to get in the Thunderbird. Stephanie hit the accelerator, and we were off. "Slow down", I said, "we do not want to attract any attention from the police." She turned her head in my direction and said, "the police are not after me". I have been married too long to recognize a conversation I was not going to win. I shut up and prayed we would get there safe and sound.

As my luck would have it, the police were posted everywhere at the train station. they were implementing a manhunt, and I had no doubt at this point who their target was. Stephanie pulled into a far corner of the parking lot to abandon the Thunderbird. "Here is where we part ways, whatever your name is." "I do not want my daughter around anything you might be involved in." She made sense, remember, the fastest way to travel is alone Plumb. "Is my disguise ok?" I asked her. "Perfect, if ugly old woman is what you are going for," she replied. She smiled, thanked me once again for the funds to get them on their way and disposing of Baby Daddy. And with that, we parted ways. Good luck girl, I thought, pick a better one next time.

I grabbed my cane, hunched a little bit to help the illusion of my secret identity and headed for the will call booth. I tried as best as possible to walk in between parked cars so I could be as inconspicuous as I could be. That worked until I got to the point where crossing to the departure side of the station meant exposing yourself all the way to your train seat. To get there undetected was going to take an Oscar winning performance. Roll tape, Action! I started towards the crossing area, and noticed at least four uniformed police officers at the entrance. They were more standing around with their thumbs in their gun belts, looking at all the women walking by rather than being proactive.

I thought that if I were walking with a group of people rather than alone I would have a much better chance of blending in and slipping by unnoticed. Slowly making sure one foot went in front of the other while my heart was pounding in my chest was a chore. Please do not bring any attention to yourself Plumb, that theme was the recurring message in a loop in my brain. "Hey!" a voice called from my left side. Surely they cannot mean me, and I took another step or two. "Ma'am", the voice said, I slowly turned my head and one of the officers was directing his attention toward me. I need to see your boarding pass mam, we are checking everyone this evening. I opened the bag John gave me, and found my train ticket along with the identification she supplied to me. "Do not piss on yourself Plumb, this is not the time to get squirrely", I thought. I extended my hand out to the officer and gave just a slight grin, he gently took my offering, glanced over it and handed it back to me.

"Have a nice trip mam", he said. I took the information back from him, placed my other hand to my mouth, fist closed, and coughed. I hoped this would be enough to not have to talk, and just nodded my head and continued on my way. First thing I was going to do when I got on the train was going to be to sit on a toilet and let it fly.

At the ticket booth, I gave my information to the clerk at the window, and she said, "You are good ma'am, just go to platform two and board the train." At least her name tag said, "Kelly", it was nice seeing another name besides John. Well, that did not last long, when I reached platform Two, the conductor waiting at the boarding station was none other than "John". Not the John that ran off with my family, and I did not think it was merely coincidence, but this John paid no attention to me once I boarded. It was going to be a 439 mile trip to Palatka Station in Florida, but that is where my boarding pass said my final destination was. Time to find my berth and find that toilet seat.

XV

The toilet seat was not the only thing inside my compartment. On a whole, my room was more like a studio apartment built for Tom Thumb. It felt like it was about ten square feet of usable space. I removed my dress and tried as best I could not to disturb my wig, and sat on the throne in my room. When I looked across at the loveseat size sleeper, There was a small gym bag and a manilla envelope seated on the wall side of the seat. After seeing that, my bowels dumped like I had the most lubricated colon in the world. Truly I hoped the plumbing aboard this train could handle the stress I laid upon it as that stress had been laid upon me.

When I was done exhaling and ready to see what was in the bag and envelope, I stood, washed my hands, splashed water on my face and sat down on the seat next to the next enigma that awaited me. I looked inside the bag, and there was another disguise for me to conquer. This time at least I did not have to be a woman. There was hair color, gray, thick rimmed glasses, that were just glass, fake teeth and a black and gray porkpie hat. "Look under your seat", was written on a blank piece of paper in the bottom of the bag.

Underneath the seat was a garment bag, with an envelope protruding slightly from an unzipped pouch section of the bag. I pulled out the garment bag, and the first thing I did was look in the envelope. Inside this compartment was my new boarding pass, Florida drivers license, and a confirmation number to a rental car company, Hertz, in Atlanta, GA, and the credit card I would need to confirm my reservation. There was also $500 for "just in case" money and a small note:

"Throw the old lady clothes out the window along with everything else in this room, do not come back here"

Once my disguise was complete, I thought I looked like Peter Falk in "The Princess Bride". I left my room, secured the door and walked out with my head bent slightly and slight shuffle to my stride, I prayed this would be enough not to attract any attention to myself. Without any incident, I made it to the dining car and sat quietly by myself hoping to have a sandwich and a cup of coffee, nothing fancy.

Sitting across from me to my right, was a man about 60 years of age, bald on top and thick horned rimmed glasses. He was streaming CNN on his laptop computer, and there was my face, being broadcast nationwide for being a fugitive in the shooting of a police officer. My appetite did not stand a chance. I sat there, in a trance like state, listening as best I could, tuning everything else out around me, "Sir!" I came back to reality to find my server looking at me as if I were deaf. "I am sorry", I said, "in another world". I gave my order, waited for him to leave and tried to resume my eavesdropping, but the gentleman and the laptop both were gone. "Great Plumb", I thought, I really did not hear anything tangible for me to use as information that might aid in my get way, just that my ass is wanted. When my order came, I asked my server if he knew where I could get a newspaper onboard, he told me that he would bring one to me. I figured I needed something to pass the time. It would be at least 200 miles to Atlanta, I would have to keep myself occupied. I was left with no other choice I would have to figure out their next move, what would be the guild's next move, well let's think here Plumb.

My paper came, and I thought it best to do what normal old men do, shut up and mind their own damn business. Most people did not want to be bothered by old people anyway, or so I believed. "What'cha reading mister?", a quiet voice came from behind the front page. I looked around the paper and saw a cute little boy about five years of age. He was a blonde, bright blue eyes and a smile that could not help but warm your heart when those dimples winked at you. "Over here son, leave the nice man alone", said what I assumed to be his mother. I smiled, waved hi to him and he scampered back to his mother. "Sorry", she said, "he loves to talk". "No problem", I replied, and resumed trying to read my paper. "It's just because he has no father figure", she said. Now I knew where the boy inherited his gift for gab. We talked the entire trip, Nathan too, that was the boy's name, I now knew more about this stranger than anyone should. From her personal life to her current situation, it seemed like this was my time to be the world's counselor, I really did not need that.

By the time we were within fifty miles of Atlanta, my migraine was making a huge comeback. I had to take some Tylenol to relieve the pounding in my brain, that was my headache. If life was going to be consistent, within thirty minutes I would be hugging a toilet, releasing the tension that had built inside me. I was thinking to myself, "shit, I can't go back in the bathroom. The note said not to, but what choice did I have. I had to puke. So regretfully I had to get up and go to the bathroom. As I was walking to the bathroom, I passed by my new friends Nathan and his mother Brooke. I had to brush them by, in order to subdue the migraine and prevent it from becoming more agitated. I started to make my way down the hall of the train to the bathroom when I noticed something odd. There was a man investigating the bathroom, he was in a suit, a very nice suit. The kind of suit that screamed government, and to make matters even worse he had in an earpiece. The fact that these guys think those things are invisible really cracks me up. It's kind of like a giant sign that says, "Hey look at me, I have someone in my ear feeding me information about something." I looked for a name tag and saw none, he didn't look like a John or anyone from the Guild. I was left with little choice, I had to stomach the throw up that was coming up my esophagus and go back from whence I came. I started to turn around and creep back to my car when the man turned and saw me. He said something into his ear piece, muffled I couldn't make out exactly what he said. But it could not have been good. He was right behind me by the time I had reached my car, luckily the boy saw me and ran up to me again. Giving me a great look of a Grandpa in training. I assumed this identity and played it off, just how my Grandfather would have done.

I picked up the little boy and placed him on my knee as I sat down. He looked a little flustered but he went for it, and so did the mom, she thought it was rather adorable. Even taking out her phone to take a picture, damnit Plumb, no pictures I thought. But it was too late, she had snapped the photo. The Government man stopped at the car and peeked inside to see what was happening. Instantly Brooke said, "Can I help you?", she snapped. Guess she had something against younger men, haha. The Government man looked around for a second, turned and went the other way. "What has happened to our privacy!", she shouted, "I hate the government." "Do not get me started, please", I replied.

"Please start", she said, "I feel like there is nothing I can do, we are all powerless. How come the rich get to stash millions of dollars in offshore accounts, tax free, but heaven forbid you or I owe the IRS a penny". For some reason the migraine began to subside, as I began to explain how important her vote was and why the small elections matter the most, she saw the importance of knowing how to cast your support for the candidate that best mirrors your own social beliefs. Not Socialism, but our society, and the best way to represent it, not the money coming in from the Koch brothers, that pour millions of dollars into elections all around the country. "It is not right that someone from not in your particular voting district can influence how laws are passed where they do not live". I ended it there, and she vowed to "follow the money" and vote for the candidate that primarily takes the interest of his or her voting constituents before anything else. "You are on the way to becoming part of the Democracy, congratulations".

Maybe it was getting back in the flow of engaging and educating people on the power they have, and why it is necessary to get involved, but the migraine was gone, and I hoped for good.

"You sound alot like that professor the police are looking for", she said. "Well, the guy makes sense, I am just glad it's not me they are looking for". She stared at me for a second, smiled and said, "yeah,I do not want them after me either".

One thought crossed my mind, when I boarded this train as a woman, I wanted to blend in with the crowd, I had a built in crowd in front of me so I went out on a limb and asked Brooke, "If something is going on, maybe it would be best to stick together." What I got was not what I expected, she beamed at me and threw herself at me, giving me the biggest hug I ever had from a stranger. Maybe we were not strangers anymore, we now shared a common foe, Mr. Government Suit. That is just how I thought of him, kind of like Mr. Agent. Then it hit me, those guys were on my trail from Durham. That pinpoint shooting that John displayed was my opportunity to escape. I NEED TO GET THE FUCK OUT OF HERE! I asked Brooke her final destination, and she told me she was going to Kissimmee. There were jobs there, not great paying ones, but there were lots of tourist attractions there and where there are tourists there are jobs. She said she could easily get a job and that the schools there had a very diverse curriculum and they had a great learning environment for Nathan.

"Safety in numbers", I thought, "How about I give you a ride in a car to Palatka Station, and you take the car from there to your destination." She looked at me not knowing what to say. "Let's just say I can afford to pay it forward." Tears began rolling down her cheeks, at that moment I could tell if anyone needed a break she did. "Just drop it off at the nearest Hertz where you are going, the charges will be on my card". Well, the Guild could afford it anyway. I was confident that an organization aimed at helping those that were innocent would extend the courtesy to a damsel in distress, and play the role of the Good Samaritan.

There goes another $500, I handed it to Brooke as a gift, a small donation to help her get on her feet. "We are all in this together", I told her, "no strings, just pay it forward when the Lord gives you the chance."

XV

I never even looked at the name on my driver's license the Guild provided me. I opened my wallet and looked at my new identity, John Smith, very original. Good thing I decided to look, Brooke asked me, "What name am I supposed to use to say thank you?" I chuckled and said, "John".

As we neared the Atlanta AmTrak depot, I noticed uniformed police at the train exit. "Ok, let's stick together and be a family so we can get out of here as fast as possible. I had no luggage, and Brooke only carried a huge duffel bag with all their worldly possessions. "I will carry the bag, and you get a cab for us". Surely a cabbie would pick up a single mother with an old man, if we were fortuitous, we would be on our way and disappear in this metropolis. As we tried to exit, uniformed police approached us and asked for our identification. "We are checking everyone getting off this train, sorry for the inconvenience", I just nodded my head and kept shuffling along. Brooke said, "no problem", smiled and continued along with me. We walked to the curb and Brooke hailed a cab. Right on cue, a cab came to the rescue. The cabbie opened the trunk and put the duffel bag in for us. After we were in, I looked at the name on the cabbie identification card, and it said "Brian". It felt good to get to some normality. To the nearest Hertz car rental please.

Within minutes, we were at our destination, I gave Brian a twenty dollar bill and thanked him for his help. He graciously accepted the large tip, removed the bag from the trunk and was on his way. I picked up the duffel bag, and we all walked inside. I walked up to the counter and asked the man at the counter for a car. He asked whom the car was under and I said "John". He went behind him and grabbed a set of keys, "here you go, oh and there was also a note that came with it". "Thank you", I replied, as I took the note I looked down and looked at the note, all it had on it was a one word phrase "enjoy". As I began to look back up from the note I heard this loud exhaust begin to spew as a beautiful car came around the corner. Glimmering in the sun, coming around the roundabout in front of Hertz was possibly the most gorgeous car I had ever seen. It was a Gunmetal Grey Mercedes Benz with matte black concave rims with red brake calipers, everything I had ever wanted in a car. The man driving it stepped out and said, "Mr.Smith, your car is ready". I was overwhelmed with excitement and I was overcome with paralysis due to it. I couldn't wait to see what was in store for me, I was like a kid in a candy store. I was brought back to reality when Brooke gave me a nudge and said, "Are you ok?" I had returned to earth. "Yeah, I am fine" I replied, "Let's get moving". Brooke, with her son waiting eagerly to her side asked, "Is it ok if we came with you Mr. Plumb?" I was in shock, how could she possibly know who I was. Had the disguise failed and had she seen through it, was this the end of the road?

Before I could even give an answer she was already entering into the car. "Are you coming?!" She yelled. Well Plumb it doesn't seem like we are left with much of a choice now are we. I proceeded around the car and thanked the man that had delivered the vehicle for doing so. I had to subdue my excitement for the time being while I tried to figure out what the hell was going on.

I got into the car, trying to be observant as possible, by this time Brooke had put Nathan in his seat belt. I asked, "are you sure he is going to ok back there?" She looked at me with a stern look and said, "Plumb he is 5, he's not an infant, plus he takes from the dick head of a father's stock." I guess he must have been a well built man because this kid looked like John Cena and Hulk Hogan had a kid. "How do you know my name, I need to know before we even consider moving." She looked at me with a very interesting emotion, it left me a little dazed and confused. "What?", I asked her. "What do you mean what?! Professor, do you really not know who I am. I knew who you were the minute you came onto the train, even in both of those ridiculous outfits." I tried to think as quickly as I could on who this woman is and then it hit me. She was a former student of mine, that blonde hair and quick wit really made a lasting impression. She was always voicing her opinions in my think tank, come to think of it I remember she was friends with Erica. "I remember you", I said, "You were one of my students". "Yes!", she exclaimed "why on earth did that take you so long". "I am sorry, I have just been rather preoccupied and my brain has been scatter brained", I replied. Geesh

Plumb, just spill it all out there huh. "I bet, especially being on the run Mr.Plumb, standing up to the Government isn't easy". Apparently word about my subpoena had surfaced on the news, especially after shooting that cop. Those reporters had their jobs for a reason, they can dig like a mother fucker. I returned my attention to Brooke when I heard Nathan in the back say, "can we go now please", the best way a 5 year old could. I turned around the seat and said "of course bud, sorry your mom and I were just catching up". Shit, I had totally forgotten that there was a child in the back seat. I went to put the car into drive having absolutely no clue where we were going. We started to pull away from the Hertz rental car center when the car's blue tooth started ringing, I looked down at the GPS to look at the caller I.D., shocker on that one...Unknown. It rang about two times when Brooke reached over and answered it for me before I even had the opportunity to do so, I looked at her with a stern look. Why had she done that? This wasn't her escape. Anyways, there was no one on the other line, complete silence until finally brooke said "Hello can we help you?". Over the blue tooth came a voice, which sounded a lot like you guessed it John. "Who is this?, Plumb don't tell me you took the girl from the train." I chimed in before Brooke was able to say anything, and surprisingly Nathan was being one of the most polite 5 year olds that I have ever met, good parenting at its finest, thank god. "Is this John?", I cut in, "Yes" he replied. "Okay good, listen John I didn't want to take the girl and boy, but I thought about it and decided they would be a great distraction by playing the "family" card."

                        I turned to Nathan and Brooke and said "Sorry, I really didn't". Brooke instantly became irate and looked like she was about to pop a blood vessel. But hey she jumped into my car, I had no idea whom she was at the time and what were the chances that she was one of my former students. I returned to the conversation with John, "Ok John, what's the plan?" What is the next move?" "That's why I called, I'm uploading it to your GPS now. Follow the route and don't make any stops." "Ok" I replied, "Oh and one more thing Plumb, don't bring anyone else into this." Before I could even respond the line had gone dead, but as promised the route had been uploaded to the GPS. We proceeded along the highway loop-out of Atlanta and headed southbound on Interstate 75. The voice over the gps said to continue along this route for the next thirty miles, then merge onto Interstate 16. It was evident there would be lots of explaining for this thirty mile part of the venture. For both of us.

        She began the questioning,since I was the one that was wanted, I felt it best to ease her mind so she would not entertain thoughts of turning me in for a reward or something along those lines. The first thing she did was tease me for not recognizing her sooner. "After seeing the press conference you did and Erica being there in official capacity as a journalist, I can understand why you would be on the run. But why shoot a cop?" When I explained what happened, and that I was innocent, she looked like she believed me. Come to find out, Brooke hated the cops because they did nothing to protect her from the sperm donor that was Nathan's father.

"I like how your real friends treat you", she said, "this is a very nice car." "Guardian Angels are real", I told her, we both chuckled a little, Nathan was sound asleep in the back seat as we rolled down the highway. I did not want anything happening to a child because of me, "Please keep us safe Lord" was the rhythm now running through my brain, I had no idea where Mr. Agent and his men were. Did we give them the slip at the train station? Are they following us? Are my wife and child alive and safe? Praying was the only thing I had control of really,and I knew I had to concentrate on the road and let God be my strength.

Out of nowhere, Brooke laid a bombshell on me, "You know Erica and I used to mess around in college". I snapped my head to the right so hard i felt a nerve in my neck pinch, sending a shockwave up to my brain. It made my eyes water a little, and I rolled my head trying to get my balance back in my head. "College is for experimenting", I said. "That is one thing I do not get about Republicans, they feel their rights are being infringed upon because someone has a different belief or lifestyle" I told her. It was really none of my business to know this, but I guess seeing her on the television recently brought back old times for her. "The real truth is that they want to use government to restrict your rights". Brooke looked at me and said, "Isn't that the truth".

She let out a big sigh and looked at me, "Thank you for not judging me". "Not my job", I told her. We smiled at one another and drove in peace until the GPS came over the car speakers and said, In two miles, take exit to merge onto I 16 south. I made sure the cruise control was set to the minimum speed limit as not to bring any attention to ourselves, but what was I thinking, we were in a Benz. I am glad I stayed in disguise, there were troops parked along the shoulder before the interchange and I really did not want to be recognized. Even if i tried to run from them in a pursuit, you can never outrun the radio. We merged onto Interstate 16, and the GPS came over the speakers again and said, "continue the route for the next one hundred fifty nine miles". That is about two hours I thought to myself, I wonder when we'll have to stop for gas.

"Was it worth it?" Brooke asked. "What do you mean I asked?" She lowered her head and looked at me exposing the white of her eyes from underneath her blue eyes. "Starting up all this ruckus", she said. "Well", I said, "If it gets people aware of what is going on and drives them to the polls to get rid of Republicans at every Municipal, City, County, State and federal Representatives out of the way of obstructing government in the course of its obligations to the people, and justifying their own discriminatory legislation that makes it harder for people to vote, then it's my belief that change will come about and it will be peaceful."

"I always thought you had grandiose thinking professor, but at least it's a humanitarian way of thinking," she said and laughed at the same time. "I also respect you for it", she said. "Mind if I take a nap for a while, this is kinda nerve racking", I chuckled and said, "tell me about it". "Get some rest, I will be up for a while", and with that, she cocked her head to the right to lean it against the shoulder strap, and closed her eyes.

I used this time to say my Daily Rosary, and meditate to Pooler, where I would pick up Interstate 95 south. As we neared Pooler, I noticed the gas tank was still on "F". What kind of car is this I thought, when they said do not stop for any reason, they meant it. That was until my stomach grumbled rather loudly, and I realized I needed sustenance. Then a voice from the backseat came alive and said, "I'm hungry too mister." There was no way I planned on traveling with a hungry child, so I woke Brooke up and informed her Nathan was awake and hungry. "He's right mom, I am", Nathan chimed in, "Ok, hold on baby and we'll get some food for you". "Ok", he said, I'll be your trooper".

Same as always, there was a State Trooper parked along the shoulder as we began to merge onto Interstate 95 south, as the GPS directed. As we merged onto Interstate 95, there was another State Trooper along the shoulder once we were in the flow of traffic. Maybe this car had stealth, I thought to myself, no one is bothering us. "Hello professor", came over the car speakers, it was John. "Go to the Subway at your next exit, let Brooke go inside and get everyones order, pay cash. You and Nathan stay in the car, do not turn it off". "Is it possible for me to talk to my family John?" There was a slight pause that made my heart do somersaults in my chest, "Very soon, remember, do not delay." Our connection was lost and Brooke looked at me with empathy in her eyes. "Oh my God professor, are you ok?" My eyes watered, but i was able to hold back the floodgate of tears that were trying to show themselves. "I'll be ok, let's just get food and go where the GPS tells us." We pulled into Subway and followed our instructions to the letter. Brooke got out of the car, and ran inside to take care of business, then Nathan let his presence known again, "I have to use the bathroom." Perfect timing I thought, he's going to shit or pee or both in the backseat of this car. "I can not turn the car off buddy, can you wait for your mother to get back?" Stall tactics can sometimes work if you try to make yourself hold it, but in those times you can not…"No, I gotta go bad." I had one chance of catching a break, if he just had to pee, I could let him pee outside the car door and let him take care of business, if he had to take a dump…"I have to do number two." My lucky streak continues.

I told Nathan to unbuckle his seatbelt, which he was able to do rather easily. I figured I could keep the car running, stand right outside of it and let nathan run inside and tell his mother. Perfect, now I had to go myself. At least I knew I could wait for Brooke to come out with the grub before it would be too late for me. "Run inside and tell your mother you have to go Nathan." Did not have to tell him twice, he was inside so fast you might think he was a track star. Staying out of the car and standing made it easier for me to hold it, but I did not want to keep my head exposed too long in case someone might recognize me, disguise or not.

Brooke and Nathan came out after about ten minutes, and I ran inside to void my bladder. Once I was alone, the tears returned as I thought of Laurie and Gabby. I did not even try to stop the river that ran down my face. The one thing I would not let myself do was let anyone hear the emotions that were running through my veins, this one was for me. When I was finished urinating, the tears subsided and I knew I better collect myself before anyone sees me this way. I did not need any attention focused in my direction. While I was at the sink washing my hands, I looked in the mirror and noticed my eyes were red and puffy, but more importantly, that bout of emotions caused the gray dye in my hair to start running down my forehead and sideburns from the sweat that ensued in the heater that was this public restroom. I grabbed some toilet paper to dry my head because there was no paper towel dispenser, they had one of those air dryers for your hands to help save the ecology. Great timing to be eco-friendly, haha.

When I opened the door, there was an elderly man getting ready to walk in, "You ok mister?", he asked me, "you look a little green around the gills." I continued dabbing my face so I would not rub and gray color around my face and said, "Yeah, lost a fight with a tuna sandwich." I lowered my head and kept on stepping, too close for comfort that encounter, get to the car and keep moving Plumb! "Watch where you're going asshole!", a woman said, I guess I almost knocked her down with the door when I went outside in such a hurry. "I am sorry ma'am", I said as I blew past her, I got in the car and we hit the road. She continued to yell obscenities at us from the rear view mirror, and I figured if there were a time when I needed a laugh it was now. I chuckled watching her reach an almost aneurysm as she yelled at us letting me know she thought I was number one by showing me only one finger.

Interstate 95 was a kind onramp, we merged into traffic and I accelerated to the speed limit and set the cruise control. I always assumed I would be getting off the train in Florida at the Palatka Station, but with the twists and turns this adventure had taken, anxiety started to creep into my subconscious and it felt like I was driving on a treadmill, just waiting for John, or the voice on the GPS to tell me my destination. One thing I guessed, we were still going to Florida since there was no Georgia driver's license waiting for me. All of us ate our sandwiches, and Nathan asked the typical road trip question children always ask, "Are we there yet?" I tried to think of something, but Brooke beat me to it, "Go to sleep baby, we are going to be in the car for a long time."

Good answer I thought, but the mind of a child does not
measure time like an adult, "how long is a long time?"
This time I was ready, "Do you go to school buddy?"
Redirect, always a good interactive distraction. I used to,
but mom said we have to move, so now I do not have a
school." It can be hard on a kid moving, losing friends,
neighbors and a community they are used to. Brooke cut
in before I could even respond "Nathan's home schooled.
I felt that he could receive a better education from home
then from a public school system. A public school system
that year after year receives severe tax and budget cuts.
How can I expect my child to receive a good and fair
education when the school he is attending cannot even
afford paper? Let alone pay their teachers a fair and
livable wage". I couldn't believe myself "Well I bet we
will be in the car about the same time it took for you to
start school and school ends, about six hours or so."
"How long is six hours?" Time for Brooke to volley this
one across the back seat, " six hours is about how long
you watch cartoons on the weekends." That one got him,
he got comfortable and nodded off.

"You will be on the road approximately 375 more
miles professor", John's voice came over the speaker.
"How can I reach you if I have a question." "I will
contact you shortly before you get to Port St. Lucie." I
got very agitated and started clenching my jaws, "You are
going to give yourself a tension headache if you keep
grinding your jaws together." She was right and I took in
a big breath and slowly exhaled. I had to repeat that
cycle for a few times before I regained composure. "375
miles, that puts us about six hours, at least I have a

general knowledge of our destination." I continued along the road and tried to begin to think of ways to keep both Nathan and Brooke preoccupied.

Once the atmosphere in the car was tranquil, I finally asked Brooke, "Why did you feel the need to tell me about Erica and yourself?" She had a far away look and grinned, "I really can not tell you, just blurted out. I guess seeing both of you on the television during that press conference, turned into fiasco, it brought back memories of how sometimes our think tanks would get a little passionate." "Yeah" I said, "They did get heated once in awhile." Brooke turned her head to look out the window of the passengers side, "It's not likely I'll ever see her again anyway." I had no idea what to say after that. It was painfully obvious it meant more to Brooke than it did to Erica, at least that was my impression.

By this point I admit I was getting a little nervous, when I looked at the gas gauge, the needle was still pointing at "F". Certainly the needle must be malfunctioning, because no car has ever performed with the miles on a gas tank seemed to be endless. We were nearing Jacksonville, FL, when John came over the car speakers, "Professor, there is a switch inside the glove compartment, flip it." When I did, the noise to the engine vanished, but we continued along at present course and speed without interruption. "That switch activates a simulated car engine sound, so it will not look suspicious when it drives by anyone. "This is a solar powered car." My heart leapt in my chest, "you mean this technology really exist and the transportation industry still mass produces internal combustion engines?" I was happy to be experiencing this new found tech that I had only dreamed possible when John replied, "the oil and gas industry has a stronghold on Washington D.C. professor, you will find how life can be so much simpler and friendly to our planet soon enough." Now I felt like a kid in a candy store, maybe I would get to meet Willy Wonka. This car is equipped with the same technology used by Tesla in their electric vehicles. What we have done is used the technology they invented called the "Tesla Power Wall".

"I've heard of that", Brooke said, "I saw it on a YouTube video once. They developed this battery that can store solar energy to be used when the sun is not out." I was impressed, I gave Brooke a thumbs up and John replied, "exactly". he refused to elaborate any further, just that we should travel now as silently as possible, and do not speed. I thought to myself, those greedy bastards, making billions of dollars in profit per fiscal quarter, and still receiving my tax dollars in corporate welfare. I was going to now thoroughly enjoy the toy that I was now driving.

"They are killing the planet all in the name of greed, I refuse to lose faith in my fellow Americans and pray they all realize that one of the seven deadly sins "greed" will have a major role in making us on the endangered species list." All I could do was shake my head and think that I am sitting in the technology that could start the reversal of the destruction that is climate change, but greed is winning at the moment. "It is not right that this is what they think, and it is alright to leave this world in worse shape than we had it when we pass it on to our future generations". Brooke chuckled this time, "Yeah, why are we left to deal with the mess Bush left us with after he and his neocons lied to the American people about Iraq." I looked at her, smiled and said, "all you have to do is watch Fahrenheit 911, by Michael Moore, you will understand why the world community want him at the Hague to answer for war crimes against the Iraqi people." "That coward will never go willingly, none of them will, Cheney, Rice, Rumsfeld, Rove, Wolfowitz, none of them."

"Have you ever seen John McCain in multiple pictures with the head of ISIS?", I asked Brooke. "No", she said, "have you?" "If you pay close attention to world events like I do, you would have noticed on CNN." Her eyes widened and she replied, "No way!" "Yes", I told her, "and he was calling them rebels that we need to arm and train to help defeat Assad." With the look of dismay, anger and repulsiveness rolled into one, she said, "How do you know that was the head of ISIS?" "It's all over the news as to who this guy is Brooke, he's not hiding."

"Preach", said John over the car speakers, "your sermons inspire me professor."

"It is very simple", I said, "they do not care who wins, they sell weapons to all sides, and whoever wins is your friend." "The thing is, if you arm everyone well, then you can drag out arms sales indefinitely."
"Very succinct and very true professor" came John over the speakers, "you have an eloquent way of making a point."

"Thank you sir", I replied, "see where it got me?" That was the first time I heard John laugh, he let a small burst of laughter out then regained his composure quickly. "Just wait professor, you have not seen where it has gotten you yet." That continued to arouse my suspicion, but there would be no sanity for me until I knew where my family was. "When can I talk to my wife and daughter?" "Right now it is safer that remains a mystery professor, we can not risk anyone finding your whereabouts until the time is right. But trust me, they are safe." John had taken care of me this far, I still had no choice but to trust him. The alternative would land me in front of a firing squad.

The speed limit dropped when we entered Jacksonville, and I complied with the speed limit. Good thing too because the cops were out in force. I also noticed revolving billboard with my face on them with a $100,000 reward for information that would lead to my arrest and conviction. Life on the run is not glamourous. As we were driving through Jacksonville, I was reminded of how small a child's bladder is, and how the rule of nature is when someone wakes up, "I gotta pee bad mister." Immediately John came over the speakers, "Not here!" I turned my head to ask Nathan if he could hold it, but I saw he was holding his crotch trying desperately to be a big boy. Naturally I did not ask that question but instead said, "Hold on buddy, let me find a cup or something."

"There is a vomit bag in the pouch behind the passenger's seat", John piped over the speakers. I figured vomit was liquid, the bag might work for urine in a tight pinch, anyway we were not left with much of a choice. "Grab the bag buddy, and pee in it." Nathan did not hesitate. He grabbed the bag and had his pants down so fast, it was cute to watch the relief on his face as he peed in the bag. When he was finished, Brooke took the bag from him, gently, and sealed the bag. Soon we would need to find a place to dispose of it, I certainly did not want to smell urine the rest of the trip.

As luck would have it, I looked in the rear view mirror,and saw the lovely color of flashing blue lights behind me from the law enforcement vehicle that was behind us. I damn near shit my pants, I said, "we are being pulled over", in hopes that John was listening and had a plan to get us out of this one. "Just be calm professor." That was reassuring for the time being. I pulled over to the shoulder, and the police vehicle pulled in behind me. My heart was pounding so hard I thought it might explode, I had no idea why we were being pulled over. I rolled down the driver's window and had the rental papers and my phony identification ready. I tried to look into my side mirror to try and see the police officer as he approached but he had a spot-light on the mirror. I was blinded, I waited patiently waiting for the Police Officer to come up to my driver side window. Finally there was a break in the light and I could finally look into the mirror to see a figure approaching the door. I rolled the window down on the driver side where I was sitting, and the officer went through the normal procedure,

"License, insurance and registration." I handed the officer my license and car rental paperwork, and he walked back to his patrol unit.

We sat in the car and waited for the officer to return to our car. As we waited, the tension began to mount within me, and I prayed the sweat would not return. When I looked at the rear view mirror on the driver's door, I saw the officer returning to my car, ticket book in hand. "I am citing you for not having the child in a set belt." That was it? I will happily sign this I thought, John Smith will never appear nor pay for this citation. He handed me the ticket book, and I began to sign my name with an "N". Quickly I tried to make the N into a J by over exaggerating the loop under the cursive line, and scribbled the name Smith so unintelligible that it would pass as bad penmanship. The officer tore my copy from the book and handed it to me. Before he gave my fake license back to me, he looked at it and the ticket, then said. "These signatures do not match". "Sorry", I said, "I am an old man and my penmanship is not what it used to be." The officer looked in the car, noticed there was a child and a woman, then said, "Make sure everyone stays buckled sir." I smiled and said, "Absolutely." He gave my license back to me, turned and started walking back to his car. I figured I was free to go, so I put the car in gear and started on my way again. I do not know if it was because the car was stealth as far as making any noises or what, but when I looked in my mirror to make sure it was safe, the officer snapped his head around in my direction and had a look of surprise on his face.

As far a I was concerned, the scope of his stop had been fulfilled. He saw a violation, cited me for it and any further detention on his part would be unreasonable as far as my Fourth Amendment rights were considered. Yet as I accelerated to merge with the flow of traffic, the officer raced back to his vehicle, slammed the door and pulled out into traffic as soon as he was able. Sure enough, he raced through traffic to bet behind me after about two miles, and put his emergency lights on again, pulling me over.

"He is pulling us over again." I said, John came over the speakers and said, "Sit tight, help is on the way." I was all too familiar with the help John and his friends at the Guild were capable of providing, but I didn't say a word as the officer was approaching the driver's door again. "You forgot your rental paperwork," the officer said. I let an audible sigh out and said, "I had no idea why your were pulling me over again, thank you."

"That was still too close," John said, "we are going to make sure you are not delayed again, as long as everyone stays in their seat-belts, got it?" "I got it", I replied. "You are about three hours to Port St. Lucie, try and stay below periscope depth." Brooke looked at me with a look that resembled, "what does that mean", and I explained it was a Navy reference, to try and stay hidden until the time has come to reveal yourself.

XVI

We kept on the freeway for some time before realizing what had happened, the cop was just solidifying his suspicions. He knew that we were not really whom we said that we were. That both our license and rental registration were both fake, he had a hunch. But now he was just double checking himself to make sure that his assumptions were one hundred percent correct.

"Punch it!" came over the speakers, "get to Palm Coast now! It's 61 miles away, do the math Plumb. Get there in 30 and I'll let you see them." Let me see who?" I said. "Your family Noah". Time felt as though it had stopped, my heart felt like it was going to pound out of my chest. My hearing was going dull from a sound in my ear that I had never heard before. What was this? I looked in front of me and my vision began to blur. With sirens now behind me and knowing what was ahead of me, there was not going to be much that could stop me.

"Slow down you dumb ass!", Brooke yelled as she hit me. I knew I could not stop though, I was so close. I wanted to talk to my family, I wanted to see my family. I told Brooke, "Would you stop if it was Nathan at the other end of what was most important?!" She gave me a look that meant she understood. She agreed with me, "You are right Professor Plumb, "Punch it, but if we die, I am going to kill you." We started to pull away, I couldn't believe it. John came over the gps and said, "Press the red button underneath the radio Plumb." I looked down and saw the button, I hesitated shortly not sure what was about to happen. I looked over at Brooke. I was cautious, I did have a child in the backseat. "I'm sorry", I said to Brooke, "I really do not know what is about to happen, but these guys can literally do anything it seems." I went ahead and finished my hands intended destination and pushed in the red button. A loud sound went off that emitted a frequency from our car. Every car in our immediate surrounding instantly went offline and stopped moving, even the cop. It seemed that we had gotten away for the time being. I looked at Brooke and said, "Well, looks like we are safe for now". Brooke looked more relieved than I had ever seen her. Nathan was crying in the back seat, and I felt at this point my migraine was coming on really strongly. A voice came back on the GPS, thank god, a friend's voice. I know what other must be thinking, how can I think of this man as a friend. The same man that had taken my family from me. Well, I thought, in his defense he has gotten me this far. Alive is a good thing. "Good job Professor Plumb, let's get you off of the road". Off of the road, what the hell I thought.

"You have to tell me what just happened John", I said. "That was an EMP professor". Electro Magnetic Pulse, this car had everything, "What doesn't this thing have", I said. "It will not sprout wing and take flight professor, but it will get you where you want to be. That sounded great, I hated feeling like I was helpless, especially when it came to protecting my family. Palm Coast was my objective, and I was hell bent on making it there.

I saw the signs for Palm Coast after another twenty minutes of driving at breakneck speed, John came over the car speakers and said, "Ok professor, this next little maneuver is going to be some on the job driver training." This ought to be great I thought to myself, "what do you want me to do, parallel parking is at the height of my driving skills." Also, having a five year old in the car did little to excite the thrill seeker in me while I was behind the wheel, "The EMP will not be at your disposal any longer professor, you will have to do exactly a I say without hesitation or question to my directions, is that clear?" I laughed so hard, Brooke looked at me like I had gone crazy, "what is so funny!", she said, "pay attention to the road!"

"There is no choice, is there John", I said matter of fact "You always have a choice professor, but is your plan better than mine?" He used my own tactic on me, ask questions and let the person come to the logical conclusion on their own, then it becomes the truth. Also, it is the best way to let someone see how to process information instead of giving lies to build a foundation on, like Fox News does. "I think the outcome will be more favorable to me if we use your method John." A little condescendingly, John replied, "They told me you were smart." Brooke got a chuckle out of that one, there was nothing for me to say, I walked right into that one.

"In the slow lane, there will be a tractor trailer rig with the logo "We Move YOU" in big red letters on the back of the trailer, let me know when you see it." I gave an audible "ok", and set my sights for this big rig. Keeping a vigilant eye in my rear view mirror also, I maintained the watch for law enforcement to be coming at me as rapidly as possible, I am sure the word had already gotten out to any aerial visual that was looking for me in hot pursuit.

And hot pursuit is what they were in. In my rear view mirror, I saw flashing emergency lights on multiple police vehicles racing from behind to apprehend me. In the distance, I saw what I hoped was my target, about three miles ahead of me in the far right lane. "There are cops in my rear view John", I said, "I am doing one hundred twenty miles per hour, and they are within view." I hoped John had a plan, and he did not let me down, "Do one hundred thirty then." Brilliant. The best answer was the simplest. I applied the accelerator to the floor, and boy did she respond. I felt my back depress further into the backrest of this solar powered wonder, and it was like accelerating through slow cars in a video game, Pole Position came to mind. The faster I went the closer I came to the tractor trailer with red writing on the back. Behind me, the police vehicles faded slightly, but not totally out of view, after all, hiding on an Interstate is a feat of impossibility.

When the red letters on the trailer came into view, it promoted something called "Zipporah", anyway, I have never heard of it.

About a mile in front of that, I saw another tractor trailer with red writing on the back of the trailer. "I saw one truck that had red writing on the back, but it was not our truck", still cruising along "John, I am really starting to freak out about these speeds you have me going." In a very soothing and relaxing tone, John asked, "What name was on the back of the truck you just passed?" I fumbled with my speech trying to pronounce the word on the trailer, "Zipporah, Zippy de do da, I can not pronounce it." Brooke spoke up without hesitation, "Zipporah".

"Perfect!", exclaimed John, get in the right lane and get off the accelerator." I did what any sane man would do with the police chasing him, I took my foot off the accelerator, got in the slow lane and decelerated allowing my pursuers to close on the gap that was my freedom. When I merged fully into to slow lane, the truck behind me had accelerated to the point where he was completely encompassing my entire view from rear view to side mirrors. The truck in front of me had began to roll up the rear door to the trailer section of the unit. I never even saw the name on the back of the trailer.

A ramp began to extend from the rear of the trailer in front of us, and I began to understand the training part of the OJT John was talking about earlier. I felt a slight bump from the rear, and felt our car being pushed along by the tractor named "Zipporah". "John, what is happening?!" I said as I felt control out of my grasp at this point, except for the steering control portion of the operation. "Listen professor, you are going to step on the gas and hold it, then brake exactly when I tell you too, got it?" Sweat was rolling down my face, and I felt my left eye burning from the salt that was in my sweat. It was hard to focus with one eye open, hoping sweat does not decide to run into it, while it was impossible to open the salt burning eye. "Got it", I said. I took off the porkpie, wiped the sweat from my forehead and eyes, and focused on the ramp that was quickly approaching in front of me.

The speedometer was decreasing,and I wondered if our gap was closing too fast. "Get ready professor", John came over the speakers, "When you feel the release from the truck behind you, step on the accelerator until both front tires are on the flat part of the trailer. Coast up the ramp and it will grab you as it retracts into the rig." He made it sound easy at least. The ramp was rapidly closing on the front of the car. My heart was pounding so hard I could feel my bladder vibrating, this was happening so fast all I could do was hope this trick worked and we would be safe under the umbrella that was this trailer.

Now here comes the moment of truth, what are you made of Plumb, can you be the hero and elude capture, or will you drive this thing through the cab of the tractor. I felt the release from the truck behind me, it felt like gliding for a second, "Now", John said. I eased on the accelerator to get enough momentum to roll onto the ramp, I had a very vivid memory of the power of acceleration this thing had. Oddly enough, I noticed the gas gauge was now at half level, amazing piece of technology. We had both tires on the front of the ramp now, just a little further Plumb, I was saying in my head. It seemed the back tires were just along for the ride, because the car never got fully on the ramp. I stepped on the accelerator a little harder, and there she went, I felt my head jerk as the rear tires finally followed the rest of the car, and I took my foot off the accelerator just as John had directed. I felt the car now being pushed into the trailer like a car on the tracks of a car wash. The light began to dissipate as the trailer door was closing, my hands were gripping the steering wheel so hard it felt like needles were being stuck in all my fingertips.

There was a "thunk" as the trailer door secured behind us, the lights in the trailer illuminated and chased the darkness and fear that was alive in the atmosphere for a second. The suspense was eating away at me not knowing if this ruse had worked we were safe again, for the time being anyway. "You are safe professor, the three of you may get out of the car and come to the front of the trailer. You may turn the key off now also professor, we have it from here." I turned the key to the off position and it looked like the "Enterprise" was powering down, I had to have one of these! we all got out of the car and walked to the front of the trailer, A panel door slid open, and we stepped through like we were on a submarine the door was so small. In the sleeper part of the tractor it looked like a mini version of the "Situation Room" at the White House. A flat screen monitor lit up,and there was John. "Congratulations professor, the posse of law enforcement vehicles has passed and we can proceed to your destination of departure." He had a big grin on his face, "now, as promised". The screen went black for a second, then when the picture resumed, there was Laurie and Gabby. All I could think was, my bride was safe and in good spirits. Tears began free flowing,she was as beautiful as ever, I could not wait to see them again.

"Baby", was all I heard, I wiped my face with my hands, smearing my face with the emotions of relief that they were safe and sound. I did not know what question to ask first, all I had the strength to do was stare at the two people that were the center of my universe. "Are you alright Noah?", Laurie asked, Gabby looked into the screen and signed, "Dad, I can not wait for you to get here!" Her expression was one of amazement and disbelief, "Where are you?" I signed, the look on Gabby's face dropped, and Laurie said, "we can not tell you yet, they said this must be kept as close to the minimum amount of information, they really are safety conscience around here, but all I can tell you is you will not be disappointed." The smile on her face is the only reassuring thing I felt after the ordeal we went through since John disabled that cop so we could get away.

The screen went dark again, I wanted to scream at it, but John reappeared and said, "sorry professor, there is something I have to brief you on so you will have a better understanding of the situation you are in." John explained why communication had to be kept brief, concise and protected at all cost. The Guild was an organization made of highly skilled, with prior top secret, intelligence experienced people, with certain special knowledge, skills and abilities, or KSAs as he put it. They were assembled from all walks of life, different religions, genders, ethnic diverse, and all had the belief that there was always common ground for people to live in an accepting and malice free society. The location of this Guild is classified,and only a very few selected people of that mindset were invited when circumstances dictate that they were deemed worthy to be made of their existence. Like my situation. Naturally, organizations like Homeland Security, CIA, FBI, etc… utilize the same technology and have the ability to expose the Guild, so John joked by saying the Guild just uses the tech better because the intended use of it as far as the Guild was concerned, was for the improvement of mankind. I knew there were things that went bump in the night I really did not want to know about, now I was smack dab in the middle of it.

We were made to feel comfortable in the sleeper part of the tractor, if sleeper section is what you want to call it. Brooke and took the opportunity to sleep,since Nathan had been sleeping for most of the journey, he was wide awake now, in a total trance at all the lights, bells and whistles that made up this compartment. From the outside. it resembled any other big rig, I guess that is what made it special. I watched the news in the tractor, seeing my name all over the screen along with my picture. Not only was my normal pic on the screen, there were artist renderings of possible changes to my appearance that may be of use to law enforcement. So called experts in the field were giving possible locations to possibly find me. Airports, boat docks, bus depots and train stations were all being heavily monitored for my whereabouts. The funny thing was that not even I knew where I was going. One thing I was certain of, either I was leaving by plane or by boat, there aren't many other alternatives having run into a backstop that was the state of Florida.

  We continued along the road in this Cab like room that resembled the situation room. I could have sworn I saw the Presidential Seal, but that might have been because at this point I was sleep deprived, scared, running for my life and at this particular instance happy. Which is the weirdest mashup of emotions that anyone can ever experience, that I know for certain. I looked over at Brooke and Nathan, whom were looking rather terrified. "What's wrong?" I asked, dumb Plumb. "What's Wrong?!" " We are running for our lives and now we just pulled a James Bond like move into the back of a trailer… And you have the audacity to ask me what's wrong? What do you mean what's wrong!?", she screamed. "Why should my son and I stay on this wild goose chase. I thought we were going to go somewhere better, somewhere where Nathan and I could have a safe some"--- before she could finish her sentence she was cut off. On the monitor in the middle of the room came a voice over the screen that caught Brooke in her tracks.

  "Hi Brooke", came Erica over the screen, "long time no see." Eyes still red from just waking up, Brooke bolted into a seating position. "How are you involved in this Erica?", Brooke asked. "There will be enough time to play catch up later, right now just know you are safe and in good hands, we will see each other very soon." Brooke looked at me like "how did you arrange this", I shrugged my shoulders and said, "I am just as surprised as you are." As far as i knew this was all one big coincidence, but then again I had to leave the possibility that it was the Guild, nothing happens this coincidentally.

"Professor, your face is on every grid and milk carton in a tri-state area. Enjoy some peace and get some rest while you have the opportunity, you are going to need it." I think she saw the blood leave my face because she said next, "remember professor, there will be no place you can show your face without being reported. There is a big price on your head." Like i needed to be reminded of that, "what is the plan then?", she looked at me like that was the dumbest question, "you have to leave the country, but to another country you will go, but not one that you have heard of." I was really beginning to hate this cryptic bullshit. "Good night professor, we will see you very soon." The screen went black and the only emotion that would not be silenced was frustration. Sleeping was the last thing on my mind, and I did not to wake in a strange place unprepared for any situation that lay ahead. Afterall, they made it seem that more turmoil and trouble lay ahead, how could anyone let their guard down and rest in a situation like this.

I was not left with much of a choice, the next thing I knew I was waking to the screen coming on as John was there with a big smile saying, "wake up professor, you are in Port St. Lucie, Florida and your final departure location is not far away. Time to wake your brain up. If you look under your cot Professor you will find a little present, remember that strain that I gave you", I reached under my cot and pulled up a little black box, I opened it and inside was a fresh joint with a note. I opened the note, and was not surprised by that hopeless romantic John.

Here is some Numb Plumb, this should last you until you are here -John

Relieved and beyond thankful for some more cerebral power, I took my gift in hand like a young boy on Christmas day. I am sure my eyes were lit, to show others just how much I appreciated the gesture. It always made me feel more perspicacious on whatever topic I was focusing on at the time. "I am stepping into the trailer for a second Brooke, be right back." She lowered her head and looked at me with a look that let me know I was not fooling anyone, "not without me she said." I opened the door, let her pass and stepped through behind her, "fire when ready professor," she said, and handed me a lighter.

XVII

The rig slowed down significantly, and was making sharp right angle turns which hinted to me we were definitely off the freeway and on city streets. "Stay in the back professor, you will be exiting through the back of the trailer." Brooke went back into the so called sleeper section, retrieved Nathan and both of them returned into the trailer section. I could surmise we were in a parking lot or something because the rig made a very big, slow right turn then came to a stop. Beeping warning signs went off at the rear of the trailer as the rig began slowly going into reverse. "We are backing into some type of warehouse I think." Brooke looked at me and replied, "you think so?" I shrugged my shoulders and said, "maybe to unload this?", and pointed at our saving chariot. At any rate we were about to find out.

There was a slight bump, at the rear, and the rig came to a stop. Slowly the rear door to the trailer rolled upward and my suspicions were confirmed, light from inside the warehouse slowly let light roll inside the trailer, and a voice called out, "come on out professor, you are among friends." I recognized it as John right away, but it was not the friends i hoped it would be, no sign of Laurie nor Gabby. John strolled towards me and had a victorious sort of look on his face, "welcome professor, sorry for the turmoil but I promise, it is better than what the alternative would have been had we not interceded." I had no response to that, John continued with something that did not make me feel victorious, "The men on your tail will not be off the scent for long, they have eyes and ears everywhere. You have no place to run but the ocean, and they know that. Every road that leads out of this state, every train station, airport, boat dock, bus depot and rental car place are alerted about you. Destroying your credit and debit cards at home was a brilliant move, at least you are not leaving a paper trail behind you."

"Glad I did something right at least," I said to John. "It is not over yet professor, we have a little going away present/party, however you want to categorize it, but that is also a surprise that we think you will enjoy very much." I looked around the warehouse and noticed lots of commotion. No party favors or things of that nature, no big cakes for girls to pop out of, no bar or food (and boy was I hungry), just people moving boxes and crates around preparing for a mass exodus or something. "Where is my family John?" It was a simple question, one I was hoping for a simple answer. And a simple answer is what I got, "they are on the island professor." Before I could ask "what island", he said, "and you will be with them very shortly if all goes according to plan." "Do I get to know that plan?" I asked, "the less you know the better, trust me professor, just follow directions and all will be fine."

Then, "Oh my God!", came from over the stacks and rows of things stacked and ready to be loaded. I knew it was Brooke, and I went running, more like trotting to her, and when I got there, after three seconds, there Was Erica standing in front of her. She stood smiling ear to ear in front of Brooke and held her arms out toward her. Nathan looked elated to see his mother so happy, as he stood grinning with that twinkle in his dimples. Erica and Brooke embraced as true old friends do. It was nice being on the inside knowledge of their friendship, and it made me feel good to see two people genuinely happy to see one another again. I wonder if being their old college professor had anything to do with re-uniting them again or if fate had any influence on them seeing one another again.

"I have a secret to tell you Brooke", Erica said. Brooke had a look like she was either a little girl getting a pony for her birthday, or someone about to have a heart attack. At any rate it was obvious she hung on the next words to come out of Erica's mouth. "I work for an organization called the Guild." I thought I was the one that was going to have the heart attack now, "you are…", "John", she said. "I made sure the two of you would meet on that train and arrive here together." Brooke and I looked at one another like we were both pawns in a game, but to what end, I still had not figured that part out.

"We agree with all of your teachings on how you should think for yourself professor and that is what has earned you your place on the island, thinking of others first and how to live the life Jesus Christ taught us to live." She turned to Brooke next, "and you Brooke, I would like the chance to see where things between us can really go, I have never forgotten you and have always loved you." Brooke threw her hands in front of her face like those were the best words that her ears had ever heard. "Of course I will go with you," Brooke said, "and Nathan?" Erica smiled at her and said in the kindest voice, "we can be a family and live without judgement."

John slowly began clapping his hands, with a big smile on his face he said, "Welcome to the family Brooke." Then he turned and shouted, "Now can we hurry up and get this thing moving, we still have to set the cameras up for the last shoot!"

The work crew began loading boxes and crates into the trailer around the car. by now the car had been surrounded by frames and shelves that resembled scaffolding, and every space was utilized for stowing the cargo that was to be loaded onto the trailer. "Follow me guys," John said, and he lead the four of us into a room inside the warehouse. There was a table set up with pizza, boneless wings, fruit and cheese, yogurt and water. "Is that for us," Nathan asked. John looked down at him and said, "I hope you leave some for the rest of them", as he poked his thumb in our direction. His smile at Nathan was genuine, very kind hearted, and sincere. Nathan bolted for the table, and I was not far behind him.

As I sat and began to eat, I could not help but stop and catch myself, what last shoot? John came to my table and sat down, "you are wondering what is happening professor, I know." Do these guys know how to read minds or what I thought. "We thought you would like a chance to go public, clear your name and give you one last opportunity to do what you do, teach!" That thought appealed to me very much, using the chance to exercise my First Amendment right of Free Speech to rail against the hypocrisy that is the way our government is being handled. "Count me in John." He smiled and gave me a pat on the back of the shoulder, "you are the man professor."

We ate in peace, and I pondered what I was going to talk about, what message needs to be given? There are so many talking points to expose and I wanted to make sure whatever was being discussed was going to be eloquently narrated, and poignant. As luck would have it, Erica came next to sit next to me. "Hi professor, sorry for all the cloak and dagger, but it was necessary in order to keep everyone safe. Remember, your voice has power, people will listen to you, especially since you are now a national figure, even if it for being a cop shooter, use it to your advantage."

I have an advantage? I wish someone would tell me what it is, came to my mind. "I will use my cover of being a reporter,and I will ask you a series of questions, think about what topics you want to cover and I will ask you them so you can do what you do best, educate." Erica got up, patted me on the back of the shoulder and walked away. I could feel the weight of truth building up inside me. The one thing reports do best is ask questions, so let her do her thing and brush up on your facts Plumb, this one will be a doozy.

XVIII

By now, the warehouse looked pretty barren. The docks were empty, the lights were off, save for a few bulbs lit strategically by the two chairs that sat in the empty space that was the warehouse floor. There were two television cameras set up on opposite sides of the chairs, and a backdrop that gave the illusion that we were in some type of office space. Erica walked toward me with a pen and notepad in hand, she really did look like a professional. "Alright professor, what do you want to talk about?" I think the most important social issues that divide this country are:

Gun control

 Planned Parenthood

 Climate Change

The right to vote

Defense spending

Citizen's United

"Wow professor, you sure want to go out with a bang." I smiled and said, "go big or stay home." "Ok professor, game time in thirty minutes."

That feeling of go big or stay home swept over me, so much so I felt everything I just ate turn to jello and screaming to let loose. This might take all of these thirty minutes, I thought to myself. I made it to the bathroom door and made it to the toilet just in time. As I sat down, it felt like an emergency valve had been pulled and everything flowed. (I know you are tired of hearing about my bowels)

I gathered myself, opened the bathroom door to exit and Erica was standing right there, "Game time professor." I took a deep breath and exhaled slowly, "I am ready."

We walked to the makeshift set and at in our chairs. Crew members helped Erica get her earpiece in, and made last minute adjustments to the cameras to ensure the best quality of ambiance would be obtained. Sweat began to roll down my forehead, and I asked for a towel to clear my brow. One of the members handed me a hand towel and said, "keep it, it will be a good prop." Erica agreed and told me, "If people see you are scared they will be more likely to believe what you are saying. It is when you are too calm that you look like there is ice in your veins and you have no compassion." Good, at least I could just be myself and let whoever was going to watch this know I was innocent. I knew there would be those stupid people that would say, "if he were innocent then let justice take its course", but those people were ignorant of how there was no escape from Mr. Agent and his kind that would allow true justice to actually work. Hell, that was the entire reason I decided to avoid the bullshit that was our bought and paid for lawmakers in Congress. That thought woke up the advocate in me, and I was ready, "Ok, I am ready," I said with conviction. Erica looked at me with eagerness on her face and said, "let's get the cameras rolling then."

She looked at me and said, "this will not be live, we will record the interview, then broadcast it from this location while we exit the building." John patrolled the set ensuring everything was just so, and looked at me with a big smile on his face. "We all have been a huge fan of yours professor. You inspired me to join the Guild with your lectures on what we call, "Cogitare". I knew that Cogitare is the Latin word for "think". That moved me, made me even more inspired to find the right words to get out in this last hurrah. I never thought that I actually inspired people to the point of making their core message one of standing up to the evil in this country that was greed.

"Quiet on the set!" John was in control of this show, and he wanted everything perfect. "Roll tape!" he yelled, and you could tell, they took this very seriously. "Action!"

Erica started in with the dialogue that would start of the interview as if she were on live television;

Erica: Good evening America, the last time I was with this man was at a press conference that went terribly violent by the hateful crowd in Durham, North Carolina. Tonight I have the exclusive with the man that is on everyone's most wanted list, Noah Plumb. Professor Plumb has agreed to meet with meet with me this evening to discuss the events that all of us want to know. The first question People want to know, Why did you shoot that police officer in North Carolina?

Plumb: Erica, I never shot anyone, I am positive the car camera from the officer approaching after the incident will prove my innocence, but I do not think Law enforcement will ever release that evidence. Truth and justice are the farthest thing from what they want you to believe, but I am innocent, I abhor violence.

Erica: Professor, if you are innocent, then why are you on the run?

Plumb: Erica, you are a professional journalist, I am sure you have seen how Republicans in Congress abuse the authority the Constitution has given them. They have used Congress try and dismantle our democracy that our forefathers have constructed. They have WASTED our tax payer dollars on partisanship politics. An example is how they have treated the ex-Secretary of State, Hillary Clinton. Everyone is mourning the loss of the four Americans that lost their lives in Benghazi, Libya. Yet they have not whispered any outrage of the thirteen Americans that lost their lives in the fifty four attacks on United States Embassies worldwide during the Bush administration. You mean to tell me four live are more important than thirteen? I do not think so. It is obvious that if Americans lose their lives under Republican leadership it does not matter, they are only concerned with smearing Democrats.

Benghazi was just partisan politics played by
Republicans. Never in the history of Congress has
anyone been questioned for eleven hours, but that is
exactly what Republicans did to Mrs. Clinton, and not
one second has been spent on the thirteen Americans that
were murdered under the Bush watch.
(I felt exuberant, and I could feel the rant wanting to roll
out of my mouth)
They had the head of Planned Parenthood under their
clutches for over five hours, and no wrongdoings were
found. They just grilled Ms. Richards because Planned
Parenthood helped women exercising their Constitutional
rights. No way I am giving them one second of my time,
they are nothing but liars and haters of anyone that thinks
differently than they do. Every Republican in Congress
and the Senate can kiss my ass.

Erica: Wow professor, where did you get the information
on the thirteen murdered Americans as you put it?

Plumb: It was an independent study done by the
University of Maryland.
Erica: That sounds like a credible source professor.

Plumb: And one you will never hear on FOX News, I

think they are an irresponsible media outlet and are
comparable to how Hitler used the media in WWII.
propagate lies and misinformation, they should be taken
off the airways for their negligence.

Erica: Let's talk about that, can you be specific with any allegations of their lies or misrepresenting of the truth to the American people?

Plumb: Well Erica, Obama has been in office almost seven years now, how much do you really want? All the lies and other mindless allegations would take more time than either of us have. But I will say that one of the biggest lies they have been promoting have been since the Affordable healthcare Act was enacted. I refuse to call it Obamacare and play into the hatred that Republicans want to label it as. They took a Republican idea, and instead of lauding it as a victory that Republicans are responsible for helping Americans, they want to dismantle it because a black man got it through instead of them. They also want to show it as a job killer, yet job growth in this country has grown since the month and year the Affordable Healthcare Act was enacted. So that lie on FOX News needs to be called out so voters can make informed decisions instead of the lies that network perpetuates. They can kiss my ass too.

Erica: What are you views on the Second Amendment?

Plumb: The Second Amendment, wow. That piece of legislation is antiquated in my opinion.

Erica: Are you saying the Second Amendment should be repealed?

Plumb: Absolutely not Erica. The Second Amendment was written over 400 years ago, during a time of revolution from the British Monarchy and British occupation. People were encouraged to arm themselves to take up the cause, at a minutes notice, to fight British occupation and have independence from the King and defend themselves against foreign aggressors. Hence the term "Minuteman" was born, and they were the Militia needed to defend this country. Now, there is no threat of foreign occupation. Our Militia is called the National Guard, and there are National Guard units in every state throughout this country. The need for the Second Amendment has changed, evolved if you will. I still believe Americans have the right to arm themselves to protect themselves and their families in their homes. There is no reason for anyone to carry a concealed gun. Anyone who thinks they need to carry a gun needs to refer to red the Gospel of Matthew, 26: 52, "He who lives by the sword shall die by the sword." In my opinion, it would be ridiculous to apply that scripture literally. As far as I am concerned, you can substitute sword for gun or any other instrument of torture and death. Notwithstanding, we already tried living in a society where everyone carried guns, and it was definitely not a safer environment, we called it the wild west, and you were considered an old man if you made it to thirty years of age. Gun violence and deaths were rampant.

I have family that have made a career in Law Enforcement, and they assure me of one indisputable fact. Having more guns does not make a community safer. The first person running to a scene as a "law abiding citizen" with a gun will be the first person shot. As a police Officer in uniform, people always know you you are. But Police never know who they are dealing with, nor what their true intentions are. The one thing a cop can do to make a community safer is when you take guns off the street.

I think the National Rifle Association is practicing lunacy thinking our streets would be safer if more people had guns. Also, the Second Amendment as it is currently written, gives government the express authority to "regulate" guns, so NRA, you can kiss my ass too. How many more people have to die before you will shut the hell up!

Erica: So you are not saying you are against gun ownership, just concealed carry, right?

Plumb: Both of those yes, but also regulate the type of weapons that are available to the public. There is no reason for anyone to have firepower like assault weapons unless you are in uniform and fighting a foreign or domestic threat. Just my opinion, but I think it is a logical solution to a problem without interfering with gun ownership rights. The word "regulate" is right there in the Second Amendment.

Erica: I am glad we are able to have this discussion without any mayhem. (that made me raise my eyebrows) Tell me what you think the issue of wage inequality in this country.

Plumb: Wow, I could go on and on discussing that issue.

Erica: Keep it simple professor.

Plumb: This is another one of those issues where FOX News and Republicans have twisted law regarding minimum wage. They want Americans to believe that minimum wage means minimal skill jobs, like fast food, hospital staff, the restaurant industry,...

Erica: Hold on professor, explain what you mean by "hospital staff."

Plumb: Think Erica, hospitals are the place where the most germs, bacteria and disease exist. Why else would people go there unless they suffered from some illness. Hospitals need to be cleaned, sterilized and maintained in a state of care that patients do not contract more illness, nor the visitors that come to see loved ones, right?

Erica: You have a valid point of reference, continue.

Plumb: Then why do the people that do those jobs of mopping, laundry, waste disposal, cafeteria, etc…, get paid below a living wage? All you have to do is go to The Library of Congress, pull up the minimum wage law and read it. Right there it specifies that the Legislative intent was so that Americans that worked full time would earn a living wage so they would not need assistance to live in poverty. Yet Republicans lie about the true intent of this law with the bullshit rhetoric about minimal skills and crap. Just another ploy to make people feel like they do not deserve to make a living wage. That is my biggest complaint. If Republicans truly were concerned about the welfare of Americans, they would stop obstructing and restricting working Americans the life they deserve and not one of poverty and squalor. None of them want to raise the minimum wage, and a good portion want to do away with the law all together so they can get away with paying less. How do these people stay in office? And more importantly, why would people want to keep electing Republicans knowing that is what they stand for. It boggles my mind how people keep voting against their own best interest.

I think the minimum wage should reflect what it would have been, adjusted for inflation, and attach it to Inflation, so the issue of minimum wage versus a living wage can be put to rest.

Erica: Do you think that is possible?

Plumb: I do, once people vote Republicans out of office so real growth in this country can be possible for all Americans. Democrats are the only one championing for the people they represent, Republicans represent that money only. Do not get me wrong, there are Democrats that are all about money too, Hillary Clinton is definitely one of the supporters of Wall Street. That is one of the reasons I like Bernie over Hillary.

Erica: We will get to that issue later, What do you say to the critics that argue raising the minimum wage will cut jobs and make prices increase on goods for Americans?

Plumb: That is another lie perpetrated on FOX News and by the Republicans. The truth is that there has not been one study, not one, that substantiates that nonsense. That is a ploy by the rich to justify not helping the workers that make them billions of for profit dollars every year. Wal-Mart is the biggest for profit company in the world, and they have the highest percentage of working people that need government assistance just to put bread on the table. In reality Erica, study after study has shown that higher wages have meant economic growth, and has been a big factor in job creation. So let's put to bed that lie.

Erica: Well professor, you claim there has been multiple studies on this issue, what credible evidence to you have to repudiate that claim?

Plumb: Look at cities that have increased their minimum wage to at least fifteen dollars per hour; Los Angeles, Seattle, New York, just to name the metropolises where the bulk of people live and where the most jobs are. In everyone of those cities, unemployment has dropped, the number of claims for unemployment benefits has decreased, so if there is another measuring stick to determine the true results of increased wages, you tell me.

Erica: None that I can think of professor.

Plumb: And this is all due to Ronald Reagan and the agenda Republicans had/have to own all the wealth in America. Correct me if I am wrong, but wasn't Reaganomics supposed to "trickle down" the wealth from the top to the bottom? You see Erica, let's just take McDonald's for an example. They made over Five Billion dollars in profits the previous year, yet they are one of the biggest promoters of the bullshit of minimal skilled jobs. The thought of a minimal skilled job force that makes billions of for profit dollars for an organization is purely greed. You cannot tell me that Four Billion in profit is insufficient, and one of those billions spread out to the working people that build that company daily is bad business. The opposite is more the case, workers that make a living wage and are treated like human beings will work harder and more efficiently the better you take care of them. So on the issue of minimum wage, Republicans can kiss my ass.

Erica: The gloves are off, ok professor. Planned Parenthood, you made mention of it earlier, extrapolate.

Plumb: On this issue, FOX News and Republicans are criminally negligent for what is happening to healthcare for women in this country. Planned Parenthood provides services to women ranging from birth control, prenatal care, pap smears and mammograms just to name a few. Only 3% of expenses from Planned Parenthood goes toward abortions. I agree that my tax dollars should not fund abortions, but I do believe women that want to pay for their own should not be denied that Constitutional right to an abortion if they choose. God gave us all free will to choose and make our own decisions, it is not for man nor government to control that. I personally feel abortion is wrong, but I am not going to stop anyone from doing what is legal. But they have fired up the psychos that go to women's health clinics, murder innocent people under the mantra that all life is sacred, yes, I think they are criminally negligent. Roe vs. Wade is the law in this country regarding abortion rights, period. We live in a nation where we live by those laws that are either decided statutorily, or judicially, that is the Constitution of the United States. It just kills me how Republicans define themselves by wanting less government, yet want to use government to restrict the entire female population in this country. Any female that votes Republican is voting against her own best interest because Republicans really do have a war on women and their rights to control their own reproductive organs. And as far as the pathetic argument, Ted Cruz(R), Planned parenthood is not in the business of buying and selling baby parts, according to the law, Planned Parenthood is allowed to recover the cost of abortions to eliminate the burden on taxpayers to pay for abortions.

So as far as Planned Parenthood is concerned, Republicans can kiss my ass.

Erica: Did you want to address Climate Change?

Plumb: That is a softball question (chuckle), scientist around the globe, NASA, and evidence of rapidly shrinking glaciers, that is a no brainer, climate change is real.

Erica: Do you think man is responsible for Climate change?

Plumb: Does a shark have a watertight asshole?

Eica: UNDERSTOOD, is it too late to make the planet safe to breath on?

Plumb: Almost. There are things we can do, and the most we can do to help ourselves is to vote out Republicans who are in the back pockets of the oil and gas industry. Elect responsible legislators that are driven to create jobs transitioning this country to 100% renewable energy. Think of that job growth.

Erica: Professor, do you really think politics has anything to do with climate change?

Plumb: Yes! You see Erica, we have the technology right now, today, to enact the changes needed to significantly reduce carbon emissions in this country. There is solar and wind energy, and that is free, so why when homeowners install solar panels do they still pay close to the same rates for energy use? It makes no sense, but it happens because Republicans control over seventy five percent of total government in this country. From the Republican controlled House of Representatives and Senate, to a majority of state governorships, state house elective bodies and municipalities, the oil and gas industry controls even the renewable energy sector. Electing Representatives that are not in it for the money would change that chokehold on America. And I believe promote the changes we need to save our planet. Look Erica, Republicans have used the same playbook, same strategy for everything that goes against what they want, and what they want is everything. That tactic used time and again is, denial. When cigarettes were found to be, dangerous, putting it mildly, they denied it. Then again they could, they had a lot of Congressmen in their wallets. When scientist over thirty year ago said our climate was severely changing due to carbon emission output, they denied it. But then again they could, they still own Congress and the Senate,and some Democrats too. Like Hillary Clinton, who was worldwide promoting "fracking" while she was Secretary of State. Fracking has been proven to be more harmful with its methane gas emission than the carbon output from internal combustion engines and power plants that pump carbon emissions into OUR atmosphere. Now she is running for President,

I really hope Sen. Bernie Sanders(I) gets the Democratic nomination. At any rate, when Fracking was proven to be catastrophically dangerous, they denied that too. Residents had to move away from their homes in Texas, (a real shit hole of a place), Pennsylvania, New Jersey, New York, anywhere major fracking was being conducted. The water became flammable when flame was put next to it (methane gas), undrinkable, unbearable, and those homes are worthless now because of the pollution now on their property, they have lost everything and having now to start over after already having built a life someplace. Look at all the earthquakes in Oklahoma due to the fracking process. But the Oil and Gas Industry is making profits hand over fist.

So yes, voting is one of the best changes we as Americans have for making change. We have a revolution built into our Constitution called the ballot box. But only 30% voter turnout is not going to accomplish it.

Greed again rears its ugly head, and voter apathy is the result of it. So on the issue of climate change…

Erica: Republicans can kiss your ass.

Plumb: You catch on quickly.

Erica: Professor, a few times now you have made negative comments on Secretary Clinton, and at the melee that was supposed to be a press conference, you endorsed Sen. Sanders. We are in a much safer environment now, please explain your views on Socialism and why we need it in America, promise no one will throw anything at you.

(They both enjoyed a chuckle at that exchange)

Plumb: Erica, in my humble opinion, and I am just one man, the President of the United States should have a reputation beyond scrutiny as far as his or her credibility is concerned. History is screaming at us, during the first year of President Bill Clinton in 1993, then First Lady Hillary Clinton was the people's champion for health care across the board for every American. Now that she is a candidate for the Oval Office, she is against that idea of united healthcare. When I look at the evidence, I see where she has taken boatloads of money from the Health Insurance industry in campaign contributions when she was a sitting Senator for the State of New York. She is bought and paid for like most politicians. That is one example showing me at least, that she represents not the people of America, but she is in it for the money. She is part of the problem.

Now, she refuses to re-establish the Glass-Steagall Act, and separate the banking industry that was a great factor to the recession in 2008. That and the illegal war George Bush#43 put us in and totally destabilized the entire middle east, but that is another can of worms Republicans want to sink us right back into. But back to Hillary. She has received boatloads of money from Wall Street too, but wants us to believe she can control big money. She has already shown how she controls the people that contribute to her, she bends over backwards to help them with legislation that makes them even more wealthy.

Bernie Sanders has no Super PAC, to support his candidacy, which means he is not beholden to the greed monster, but wants to choke it off, return living wages to the middle class, so bullshit excuses like, "you make too much", will be a thing of the past when it comes too middle class working Americans. The biggest thing, I challenge anyone to find an issue he has flip flopped on, HIllary bends like a weed in the winds, bending to the whim of whatever her donors want her to go.

I know Bernie wants a single-payer healthcare system, and I agree. But it will not happen until Republicans are voted out of the way so the welfare of all Americans are looked after, and not just those who could afford it. I think it is absolutely repulsive to have a healthcare system based on an Insurance Industry. It feels like the vultures have a lookout for our wallets, and they actually put a price on your well being, if it is worth defending or not. Having a Capitalist approach to healthcare is abominable. Think about it Erica, how fucked up of a society do we live in when we allow people to make rules that mandate we give them our money on a "what if" basis? We have allowed it to be the law with the Affordable Healthcare Act, and we set the precedence with auto insurance under Republican President Ronald Reagan. No one made a fuss when that was passed under dear old Ronny, but look at the fus made over the Affordable Healthcare Act. That means Republicans think protecting your car is more important than protecting human lives.

I know Bernie supports "Black lives matter" because he believes even more in "Black Voices Matter".

The best reason I support Bernie is because he will take marijuana off the Schedule One list of Narcotics in this country. If that is not enough to get out and vote for the plethora of candidates that support that, then we truly have lost control of the government the people want. Either way, all the politicians that get money from the Insurance Industry make out like bandits in kickbacks for making laws like this. Wake up people!

Erica: So you are calling for people to get out and vote.

Plumb: I am calling for a revolution at the ballot box!

Just then John burst in and shouted, "Out, now!" I turned and looked at him like "who are you talking about?" Erica was up and moving, she grabbed my shirt by the chest and heaved me up, "Move!" Now I knew he was shouting at me. Erica grabbed me by the arm and started pulling me away from the makeshift set toward an exit sign. "Through the back corner door!", John yelled. I went whichever way Erica was pulling me, all the while keeping an eye out for Brooke and Nathan. Why I felt responsible for them is beyond my comprehension, Erica arranged this.

From outside, sounds of helicopters from overhead were approaching, funny what you think about during stressful situations. I never thought from inside an abandoned warehouse how sound from the outside travels unfiltered inside the premises. I was like an echo chamber, and I could not tell where the sounds were coming from. Erica gave me a big tug and screamed at me, "Let's go professor!" From that point I focused on myself, thinking only of getting back to Laurie and Gabby. I swung my head toward Erica and followed her to the exit in the far corner of the warehouse. The stairs led downward about five steps, and thank God it did because i heard a loud gunshot echo from within the warehouse. There was a ricochet off the metal guardrail a rung above me, then striking the wall above and behind me causing that part of the wall to shatter where the projectile struck it. I lowered my head below floor level, and hurried out the back door behind Erica like she was a pulling guard on the offensive line. As we ran out the door, there were multiple shots being fired from inside the warehouse,I was not made for shootouts!

The back lot behind the warehouse was unlit and the perimeter was walled by chain link fence with razor wire encircling the top of the fence line, going over was not an option. Erica led me to the back fence corner where there was a gate. She opened the gate and we ran along the fence line of the row of warehouses in this commercial district. Spotlights were now illuminating from above as helicopters arrived and maintained a view of the perimeter of the building. We had just made it outside the firefight area, and we continued along the back fence line, and I asked Erica, "Where are Brooke and Nathan?" We got them out of the building before your interview, I do not want anything happening to them. I did not say a word, we both had a lot riding on getting out of here safely, so I continued to follow her lead as shots rang in the distance.

We Started to descend down the hill on the other side of the perimeter. Erica turned and looked at me as we approached a sewage tunnel. "Don't Judge Professor", I must have been making quite the face because I was not excited about going into a sewage tunnel. "As long as I get to see Gabby and Laurie again I really don't give a shit Erica", pun intended. Erica looked back the other way and began to pull me into the tunnel. Let's go, we have to hurry, they are waiting for us, I thought to myself. These guys always have a plan don't they. We entered into this steel cylinder tunnel and began to move. It actually surprised me that the smell wasn't that awful. I expected to enter a rat infested sewage drain, but what I saw was a tunnel, lit along the ceilings with fluorescent lamps and just a damp musty smell from all the water that surrounds Florida was my guess. "Hurry professor", Erica said, and she started sprinting down the tunnel. I ran, as best as a fifty five year old man can, but I was not running her down anytime soon.

After about one hundred yards, Erica was waiting for me by a door, "Glad you could make it speedy", she mocked at me. She swung the door open and the smell of salt air blasted my nostrils. There on the other side of the door was the beach about another two hundred yards. hearing the waves crashing along the shore made me wonder if swimming to safety was my only way out. By now I am sure there was a dragnet out searching for me. Erica closed the door and grabbed my arm, "Let's go, now!" It was a blessing we were crossing the beach under the cover of darkness because running in the sand was even more of a challenge. Once again, as I reached Erica, she laughed and said, "Are you a slow poke so I have to do all the work?" All I could do was bend over with my hands on my knees trying to catch my breath.

What appeared to me to be just a mound of sand was in fact something altogether different. She reached in the sand and lifted the corner of a plastic tarp revealing the front of a black rubber dingy or something. "Help me professor, grab the other end and make sure we pull back the tarp evenly." I followed along the sand line revealing the tarp and traced it to the other corner of the edge. I lifted my end, and sand began pouring off the edges of the tarp. That did not make it any better though, ever lift sandbags? This was worse because the sand continuously reshaped to make the tarp a difficult as possible to lift off the dingy. We pulled until the entire craft was finally revealed. It was a black rubber lifeboat with a first aid kit, flare gun and satellite phone. Erica went to the rear of one end of the craft and told me to grab the other end. "Lift", she said, and we both picked up the craft from the rear. "Now let's go." We began walking toward the ocean, pushing the front of the boat along the sand.

The density of the sand made it hard to push the boat. I pictured myself in the gym doing "farmer's carries", and fought through the resistance. "So this is it, I am going to be a pirate now and try and live on the seven seas." Erica looked at me with a big smile and said, "you have no idea professor." The front of the boat reached the water, and i thought the water would make it easier, but the initial contact made the boat grip the sand like it was velcro, "Heave!" Erica yelled. With the last ounce of strength I had, motivated by keeping my ass out of prison for the rest of my life, I gave one last push toward the ocean. The next tide lifted the front of the boat, and we gave another heave pushing the boat farther into the water. With each ebbing rhythm the ocean gave, we were further into the water. Now up to my knees in the Atlantic, Erica yelled, "jump in!" I jumped as high as I could, and lifted my stomach on the top of the boat. Once I was sure I was not going to fall back into the water, I swung my left leg over the side, and rolled the rest of my body into the lifeboat. Erica pushed a button and a blue light illuminated from the top of the motor.

We started under power of whatever this was pushing us through the water, and I asked Erica, "What kind of motor is that?" She looked at me and said, "professor, haven't you figured out everything we have is solar powered, and the battery source is the top of the line for storing the energy from the sun so we can still operate at night." I rolled my eyes upward and thought to myself, "duh". "We are not out of the woods yet professor, we can be almost certain the Coast guard is alerted and scouring the area for any sign of your escape by sea. We must be very quiet." Good thing we have a quiet source of propulsion I thought to myself.

There were lights off into the distance, oil platforms, cargo ships, possibly naval vessels off the coastline,at any rate I just prayed one of those sources of light was friendly.

Sure enough, spotlights approached from helicopters in the distance. Erica accelerated our speed without making a whisper to our location, except the splashing of waves against the bottom of the boat as we moved out to sea. If this was my escape, then I wanted to see what I was leaving. I turned around and looked back toward the beach. Lights were getting smaller, but I could still make out signs of police presence by the strobing of red and blue lights bouncing off buildings and windows. Escaping that made me feel better. I looked out to the ocean to see the blackness that was the dark side of the planet, with still just the flickering of random lights miles out to sea as it would appeared. Another spotlight swung in our direction, but it passed in front of us by ten feet, and continued its sweep of the waters. Yep, it was the Coast Guard, slowly patrolling the coastline in one of the smaller patrol boats they have. We made it out to sea farther than they anticipated us making our getaway via the ocean. the boats patrolled between where we were and the beach, I exhaled thinking the worst was over. I asked Erica where we were headed, and she told me, "You are going to see an old friend."

"Is anyone going to bring me to my family!" All of a sudden, a surge of anger and frustration came over me. Being forced out of my life, separated from my wife and daughter, and the home we built as a family, all three of us, just made me feel so helpless I thought I would have a stroke. "I promise", Erica said, "they are where you are going."

Just then, Erica whispered in a loud voice, "Duck!" I saw the silhouette of my left shoulder began to appear, and I threw myself to the right to hide myself from the oncoming spotlight sweep that came from behind me. The light missed the blackness of the boat in the water against the night, and we escaped for the last time any sense of danger from the authorities. Erica picked up the sat phone and pushed a button, "what exactly did you do?" I asked, "I set a signal for our location so we can be picked up, a beacon if you will." I had to ask, "Can anyone pick up this signal?" "Only if they have our exclusive frequence we broadcast on." I felt better after hearing that, and shortly thereafter, came a large yacht sized boat approaching with lights illuminated along the sides and ropes hanging from the top rails.

"Hope you have rope climbing skills professor." as we passed alongside the yacht, Erica grabbed a rope and yelled at me to grab the other one. "Wrap your leg around the rope professor!" she yelled, "and stand on the rope pinching the rope between your feet!" I held onto the rope and let the lifeboat drift away below be as I clung to the rope. "Raise your knees and keep the rope between your feet!" I saw how she did it and repeated her motion. "Now stand!" As she rose to a standing position, she ascended the rope, and I followed suit. We repeated that climbing inchworm style of rising to the top of the guardrails along the deck of the yacht.

"Climb Noah!" came a shout from above, it was Laurie. I gave no thought other than to get closer to the sound of that voice. AsI reached the top, two hands grabbed my right wrist, and two hands grabbed my left wrist. I was pulled over the guardrail and I landed on the deck of the yacht. I saw Erica hoisted over as well, and Brooke raced to her, embracing her like she had been given the biggest winning lottery ticket ever. Laurie threw her arms around my neck and squeezed tightly. Gabby jumped on my chest and gave me a huge hug. "Welcome aboard!" came from above me, there was my oldest and dearest friend, Jack.

"We have everyone on board," yelled Jack, "full speed ahead to Zipporah!" "Aye Captain", echoed the order, and Jack said, "Follow me." Erica had disappeared, and it was just the four of us, so we followed Jack. "Zipporah is the name I saw on the back of an eighteen wheeler", I told Jack. "Yeah, nifty piece of driving my friend," he said as he smiled at me. I am sure you have lots of questions and I promise to answer as many of them as I can, but let's get some real food in you."

We went into the galley, and my heart leapt for joy, there was the master chef, Jennifer. Jennifer is very special, she has Down's Syndrome, but is an accomplished chef in her own right. "You look beautiful," I told her. I held her in a bear hug because it was go good to see her, she had a beautiful smile. She prepared swordfish with couscous and asparagus, it was exquisite. Jack opened a bottle of Pinot Gris, and it was the perfect compliment to a perfect meal.

"She actually runs the entire culinary facility on Zipporah," Jack said. "That's amazing , but what is Zipporah, Jack?" He leaned forward, looked me directly in the eye and said, "Every vessel should be named after a woman, Zipporah was the daughter of Noah, the great Ark builder. It is only befitting she be given the name Zipporah, because it just may well be what mankind has to exist on if things continue along the path of hatred and greed."

Jack leaned back in his chair, exhaled, and said, "And it may be your only chance anymore at a free life, as it can be. But at least you will not be hunted there. Apparently there was a mole in The Guild, and instead of your interview being recorded, it was being broadcast live. That is why things changed so rapidly, my apologies.As I sat there the word Zipporah rang in my head. Excited would be an understatement, let's just pray nothing else happens...

Epilogue

Noah, there is something I must tell you, and it is very important because it is why you have been invited to Zipporah. You have known me since our college days, and you have known that my family was wealthy beyond measure. You know that I inherited that wealth once my parents went to heaven. Never once have you asked me for anything, a loan, handout, borrow my car, nothing. There are not many people I have encountered in this world that wanted my friendship just for who I am, and I have admired that about you since I have known you. For being my friend, let me tell you about your new home.

Now sitting aboard Jack's yacht, he begins to fill us in on Zipporah, what it is, how it operates and what its mission is. It was hard to wrap my mind around this, philosophy, for lack of a better term. Laurie and Gabby seemed to understand it pretty quickly, and the idea of Zipporah really seemed to appeal to her. It was simple, in the Book of Exodus 16, it talks about manna from heaven, and being instructed to "take only what you need", and all ate sufficiently without greed or envy.

Zipporah is a manmade island that operates in the oceans and main major, deep, bodies of water. To describe what Jack was telling us was totally mind blowing, it had a major propulsion system that allowed the island to traverse like any other sea worthy vessel on the oceans. It was totally powered by 100% renewable energy, equipped with solar, wind and hydroelectric power, not one apparatus of carbon emitting gasses existed on Zipporah. My mouth hit the ground when he told us of the solar powered helicopter that was on the island.

The mission of Zipporah was beautiful, simply to foster love, support, and empathy for our fellow man. There was no such thing as money, or currency or any other form of monetary value established on Zipporah, and the people there were hand picked for one reason or another. The selection process to be invited to Zipporah was simple, and Jack told us in third grade terms. "I was in New Orleans for the ten year anniversary of the re-birth of the city after hurricane Katrina blew through leaving death and destruction in her wake." He lowered his head for a second or two, raised it and said, "There was a play where the stage was set with only five pairs of shoes, each pair represented the disaster from a particular point of view. The beautiful thing was the five cast members took turns standing in each pair of shoes telling the story from their perspective. If all of us took the time to be empathetic and stand in the shoes of the other person there would be a lot more love and compassion in the world instead of the us versus them attitude people develop. And it is always the short-sided moron that wants to point the finger instead of providing a solution based on the fact we are all human beings and one day it might be us in a Katrina type of situation."

"Amen Jack", I said, "there is not enough empathy in the world and too much judgmentalism."

So, now you know how I got here on this island, Zipporah. It is a community where people of all different genders, religions, national origins, LGBT, fields of study, or any other point of view that offers love and brotherhood to one another.

I tried, I did all I knew what to do. I educated people on the importance of voting, and more importantly how to vote in your own best interest. But the trend continued, Democrats did not show up to the polls, not even to make marijuana legal, thirty percent of eligible voters went to the polls, and Republicans got the trifecta of owning the White House, Congress and the Senate. The Iran Nuclear deal was reneged on,war began and escalated beyond the scope of understanding and now I sit here watching Nuclear Intercontinental Ballistic Missiles flying overhead, there is no more communication from anyone we can reach, hoping for any survivors of this nuclear holocaust.

I pray somewhere someone survived.

THE END